The
Bridlington
Lifeboat

The
Bridlington
Lifeboat

Fred Walkington MBE

Phillimore

2005

Published by
PHILLIMORE & CO. LTD,
Shopwyke Manor Barn, Chichester, West Sussex, England

ISBN 1 86077 335 4

Printed and bound in Great Britain by
MPG BOOKS LTD
Bodmin, Cornwall

Contents

Acknowledgements

I wish to acknowledge the help given to me by the following: the Treasurer of the RNLI and President of the Bridlington Branch of the RNLI, Iain Bryce, who has kindly written the Foreword for this book; Sarah Stocks together with the staff of the Reference Library, King Street, Bridlington; Laura Shears of Lloyds, London; Barry Cox, Brian Wead and Helen MacHugh of the RNLI, Poole; Arthur Golding of Barnet and Paul Russell of Cromer for their help with information; The East Riding of Yorkshire Council; Marie Dick, Charles Brear, Hull Daily Mail publications and The Bridlington Free Press for their kind permission for the use of photographs; every reasonable effort has been made to trace all the photographic copyright holders.

My thanks to Michael Mortimore for his help with editing. Thanks also to Peter Frank, author of the book, *Yorkshire Fisherfolk* (Phillimore, 2002), for giving me the confidence and encouragement to write this book.

I extend my gratitude and love to my wife Carol for her unfailing encouragement, help and support in the research and writing of this book, combined with her constant love and enthusiastic support in my time as crew-member and 25 years as Coxswain of the Bridlington Lifeboat.

FRED WALKINGTON ESQ. MBE

Author's Note

All the proceeds from the sale of this book will go to the RNLI, in order to help save lives at sea.

Being a member of the lifeboat team for over 40 years has allowed me, as part of this community, the privilege to join a long list of Bridlington men who have taken part in saving life at sea.

I have made no attempt to include every detail of the 200-year history of our lifeboat. To undertake to do so would possibly mean missing out some part or person, with the chance of offending someone.

The intention is to highlight the lifesaving work carried out by the people and lifeboats of this community for 200 years, 1805–2005.

List of Illustrations

Foreword

Bridlington Bay has shown the need for lifeboats consistently over 200 years.

On a warm summer's day the white cliffs round to Flamborough Head and the golden sands stretching nearly 30 miles south to Spurn Point look welcoming and safe. However, all is not what it appears. Should the wind get up, especially in the south-east, when the tide is low or ebbing, there is no refuge available. The harbour is without water and the Bay is shallow.

This well researched and scripted book vividly describes the many instances when the wind, tide and cold darkness of the night combine to put terror into the hearts of those in distress. It also accurately recounts the many huge and humbling acts of heroism and courage that lifeboat men have given in Bridlington, generation after generation, to save lives at sea. The involvement of the many non-seagoing volunteers and fund-raisers in supporting the Station is well documented, showing the affection the town has for its lifeboat and crew.

I deem it a great honour to be involved and to be asked to write the Foreword to Fred Walkington's definitive history. His long service and 25 years as coxswain say it all, but now to be an historian and an author demonstrates, yet again, his life-long commitment to the RNLI and to the Bridlington station in particular.

Iain R Bryce

1

The Port of Bridlington
and the First Lifeboats

On a fine summer's evening, looking across the calm waters of Bridlington Bay bathed in warm evening sunshine, it is hard to imagine that the North Sea can be one of the most treacherous and hostile places in the world for ships and their crews. Overseas shipping since earliest times was mainly a result of the desire and need for trade. The geographical position of the continent to our shore induced trade from Bridlington and other ports on the east coast, and the coastal shipping trade evolved because of the poor state of the road structure in England.

As a result of the wholesale destruction of medieval documents at the time of the Reformation and later during the Civil War, little is known about the early history of the port of Bridlington Quay. Wool was known to be exported and by the 16th century it had become a port of overseas and coastal trade. The cargoes shipped from Bridlington were mainly foodstuffs and the imports mainly coal. In the 17th century overseas trade expanded to the Low Countries and corn, malt and butter were exported. The imports also increased: timber from Norway, brass and iron from the Baltic, tiles and bricks from Holland. In addition there were passengers and the weekly postal service to and from Harrison's Wharf and St Catherine's Dock, London. This coastal trade was said to be the nursery for the Royal Navy, the most famous to move from it into the Navy being Captain James Cook.

By the mid-1800s Bridlington as a port had declined, following the arrival of the railways. Transportation of goods now became faster by rail, which took trade away from the shipping industry. Bridlington still remained a harbour of refuge for the sailing ships that continued to ply their trade along the coast.

In the early 19th century 200-300 ships were reported to be sheltering in the Bay and harbour on a regular basis; in 1844, 761 ships, but this number did not count fishing vessels entering the harbour. Between 1849 and 1860 the number varied between 241 and 433 plus over 100 fishing boats from fishing ports along the coast – all entered the harbour of refuge at Bridlington for shelter.

All fishing and maritime communities had their own ideas about the most seaworthy boats. Each would have used these boats when attempting any rescue or rendering help to those in need. Along the east coast it is more than likely to have been the coble, the working platform used by fishermen along this coast since Elizabethan times.

On 1 October 1804 one such incident took place at Bridlington Quay, as the *York Chronicle* reported:

A vessel was stranded on the sands; three unfortunate mariners and a cabin boy saved themselves from immediate destruction by clinging to the mast of the stranded vessel. The sea was described as 'mountainously high,' no man was able to venture to their aid, until Col. Pitts, who was the commander of the Volunteer Corps at Bridlington Quay, with the assistance of his Lieutenant, ventured out in an open coble, at the hazard of their own lives, and saved the ship's crew.

Not until the late 18th century was any organised effort made to help mariners, who were unfortunate enough to meet disaster at sea. Sailing ships, many of them half rotten and in a poor state of repair, were completely at the mercy of the sea and weather. The ship owners had insured the boats, and the insurance was in many cases worth more than the value of the vessel. It was quite common for vessels to leave the port of departure never to arrive at their port of destination, to disappear without trace, or to be wrecked, with loss of life as the following newspaper entries record. From the *Hull Packet*:

April 1st 1805. Ship sailing from Embden, sailed bound for Newcastle on the 16th September 1804 and has not been heard of since.

March 17th 1805. The *Stranger*, Master John Richardson, from Gainsborough with the oak timber bound to Whitby, it is on the shore near Flamborough Head and will be wrecked.

February 11th 1805. The Cupid of Burlington Quay, sailing from Wales with coal is lost on the Pan Sand near Margate.

February 11th 1805. The *Jeanie Cowan* which arrived here yesterday from Norfolk Virginia. When off Flamborough Head, had the misfortune to be run foul of by the Brig *Horatio*, formerly belonging to this port. The *Jeanie* was obliged to cut it's cable to set the *Horatio* clear, which was no sooner done than the Brig sank, together with the mate and a boy, who were drowned. The captain and the rest of the crew succeeded in getting on board the Jeanie and arrived here safely.

Even stranded vessels were, if of any small value, sold off at the instructions of the insurers.

18th February 1804. BURLINGTON QUAY,
To be sold at Auction (On account of the underwriters,)
At the house of Mr. John Molden, *The Ship Inn*, Bridlington Quay, on Thursday, 23rd Feb. 1804, at Ten O'clock in the morning.
THE HULL OF THE BRIG *SURPRIZE*.
Joseph Brooke, Master, as she now lies in the harbour of Bridlington Quay, lately stranded on Flamborough Head, 130 Ton's registered. Immediately after the sale of the hull, will be sold all the materials of the above vessel, in different lots, consisting of anchors, cables standing and running rigging, sails etc. For particulars apply to Mr. Thomas Ward, at Bridlington Quay.

It was not uncommon for ships to be wrecked within sight of land and safety. Onlookers witnessed the plight of the crews falling from the rigging or being washed into the sea from the wreck, listening to the calls for help of the terror-stricken victims, who became exhausted by prolonged anxiety and exposure, as they perished in the violent, storm-tossed sea.

It has been estimated that the number of ships wrecked off the Yorkshire coast since the year 1500 is well in excess of 50,000. From 1770 to 1805, 174 ships foundered that were known about. Others out of sight of land, might have just disappeared without trace along with their crews. The disasters that inevitably occurred to the ships employed in this trade inspired men to design a boat capable of withstanding violent weather, therefore allowing the saving of life from shipwreck.

Positive efforts were made to produce a boat with good sea-keeping qualities to launch into adverse sea and weather conditions, which was a combination of ideas and the knowledge of local boat builders. The self-righting principle was claimed to be invented by Monsieur De Bernieres, a Frenchman, in 1775, when he held trials on the Seine in Paris. The Rev. James Bremner, of Orkney, exhibited the self-righting principle for the first time. He suggested in 1792 that an ordinary boat might be made self-righting by strapping in place two watertight casks in the bow and stern of the boat and fastening iron to the keel. Lionel Lukin of London, a coachbuilder, had fought against apathy and opposition to build and launch a boat to help save life. It is said to have been in the shape of a small coble. In the year 1785 the boat was put on the coast at Bamburgh, and helped save many lives.

Another man, William Wouldhaves, had a very fertile mind, turning it in the 1780s to the designing of an unsinkable boat. William did not think ship owners would go to the high cost of converting existing ships or boats into unsinkable boats, so he set to work designing one from scratch. The model he produced had a straight keel, high peaked water-tight ends filled with cork and was made of tin. The full-size boats were to be made of iron or copper. This design was at that time far too revolutionary. It is not known if Wouldhaves had heard of Lukin's patent, which is said to have been an improvement on the De Bernieres boat developed in France, but it is unlikely that either Lukin or Wouldhaves had any knowledge of the Frenchman's invention. Both Lionel Lukin and William Wouldhaves claimed to have designed the first boat, which could be called a lifeboat.

It is generally accepted that the invention of the lifeboat cannot be attributed to any individual. The ideas of a number of men, some known, some unknown, were put into practical designs, then added to as new improved ideas came along. This continues today in the fleet of the RNLI's lifeboats.

The Earliest Lifeboats

The Gentlemen of the Lawe House was a social club for ship owners and others, which was situated on the cliff top overlooking the mouth of the river Tyne. From this vantage point it witnessed on 15 March 1789 the ship *Adventure* run on to the rocks and become a total wreck with the loss of all hands. Having seen such a disaster so close to land, they offered a reward of two guineas to the person who drew up the best plan, to be agreed by the committee, for a boat to be built, to travel through and withstand the heavy breaking seas caused by gale and storm-force winds. The boat was to be used to rescue seamen from ships like the unfortunate *Adventure*, driven ashore in such wild stormy conditions. The list of specifications included buoyancy, strength and the ability to go through water with little resistance. Each end had to be the same, so, when leaving a wreck, she didn't have to put about (turn round) in a heavy sea. High bow and stern were essential to help prevent water entering the boat and a light draught was needed to suit local conditions.

The committee looked at the many plans submitted on 22 July 1789. Only two models were picked, one from William Wouldhaves, the other from a local boat builder,

Henry Greathead. The committee didn't choose an outright winner; instead the chairman, Mr Fairles, and Mr Rockwood, another member of the club, produced a model based on a Norwegian yawl and some parts of Wouldhaves's design, although the self righting capability of the boat had been omitted. The model was submitted to the committee who adopted it. The local boat builder, Mr Greathead, was invited to build the boat. His sole contribution to the design was a curved or rockered keel. The boat, named the *Original*, was launched in January 1790. It was established as the first boat to be built and used as a lifeboat on our coast. The hull of the *Original* was clinker built (overlapping planks) which resulted in a coble bow, reminiscent of a Viking long-ship. The specifications of the original were extreme length, 30 feet, length of keel, 20 feet, breadth of beam, 10 feet, depth of waist outside, 3.25 feet, depth inside to deck, 2.33 feet, stem and stern, each 5.75 feet high, sheer of gunwale, 30 in. It was made to pull 10 oars, double banked, with iron raw-locks for the oars, and had a very raking stem and sternpost 10.5 inches to one foot. The main keel measured four inches in depth, with a very considerable curvature, and three sliding keels. On each side, running fore and aft, was a cork lining 12 inches thick, which reached from the deck to the thwarts; and outside was placed a fender of similar cork material, four inches wide and 21 feet in length. Nearly seven cwt of cork was used in the construction of the boat, which gives an adequate impression of its great buoyancy. The features these early boats lacked were air chambers (end boxes), to make them self-righting, and the means of self-bailing. The cost of building her was £76 8s. 9d. She proved to be a great success.

The next boat was built for the Duke of Northumberland, whose son, fifty years later, played a large part in the development of the lifeboat service. This second boat was based at North Shields; many more orders for lifeboats were placed with Greathead. His chief patron was Lloyds of London chairman, Mr Julius Angerstein. The great influx of new members which had followed the reforms of 1800 had given Lloyds, for the first time, the command of a substantial corporate fund, and by 1803 it amounted to £43,000. Lloyds gave Henry Greathead full credit for the boats he built. An application to Parliament for financial assistance failed, but the general meeting held on 20 May 1802 voted him a reward of one hundred guineas and, on Angerstein's initiative, authorised the committee to earmark £2,000 from the corporate funds of Lloyds for the construction of lifeboats to be instituted in different parts of the British and Irish coasts. This extra work created more jobs; adverts appeared, as in the Hull newspaper, Saturday, 23 April 1803: 'Wanted, several good boat builders, all will meet with the Liberal encouragement, by applying to Mr Greathead, South Shields.'

Applications for assistance from this fund were carefully scrutinised, and the usual response was a grant of £50 towards the first cost of the boat, on one condition, that the remainder, together with a cost of manning and upkeep, should be by a local subscription.

The Founding of the Lifeboat at Bridlington Quay

In 1804 a committee from Bridlington Quay had an application accepted for the building of a lifeboat to be used at this port for the saving of life. The lifeboat cost £150, paid for out of a fund of £300 collected locally. The lifeboat was delivered

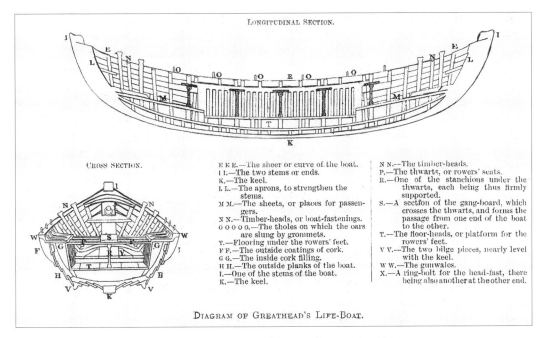

LONGITUDINAL SECTION.

CROSS SECTION.

E E E.—The sheer or curve of the boat.
I I.—The two stems or ends.
K.—The keel.
L L.—The aprons, to strengthen the stems.
M M.—The sheets, or places for passengers.
N N.—Timber-heads, or boat-fastenings.
O O O O O.—The tholes on which the oars are slung by grommets.
T.—Flooring under the rowers' feet.
F F.—The outside coatings of cork.
G G.—The inside cork filling.
H H.—The outside planks of the boat.
I.—One of the stems of the boat.
K.—The keel.

N N.—The timber-heads.
P.—The thwarts, or rowers' seats.
R.—One of the stanchions under the thwarts, each being thus firmly supported.
S.—A section of the gang-board, which crosses the thwarts, and forms the passage from one end of the boat to the other.
T.—The floor-heads, or platform for the rowers' feet.
V V.—The two bilge pieces, nearly level with the keel.
W W.—The gunwales.
X.—A ring-bolt for the head-fast, there being also another at the other end.

DIAGRAM OF GREATHEAD'S LIFE-BOAT.

1. *Diagram of Greathead's lifeboat, Bridlington's first lifeboat.*

between January 1805 and no later than March 1805. A newspaper article on 9 April 1805 reported, 'Lifeboats have been sent by the inventor, Greathead, to the stations of Cromer, Leith and Bridlington Quay also one for an East Indiaman bound for Bengal.'

This was 19 years before the National Institution for the Preservation of Lives and Property from Shipwreck, later to become the RNLI, was founded, and seven months before a fleet of warships of the Royal Navy, under the command of Lord Nelson sailing in his flag ship HMS *Victory*, fought and won the battle of Trafalgar.

Later, on 22 June 1805, Lloyd's of London paid to Mr Allan, of the lifeboat committee, for a lifeboat already established at Bridlington Quay, Yorkshire, a subsidy of £50, towards the cost of the lifeboat the Committee had bought from Mr. Greathead of South Shields.

The harbour was described as being situated at the mouth of a small stream, the Gypsy Race, which flows across the Yorkshire Wolds into Bridlington Bay. The harbour is sheltered by low cliffs to the north, and had been a natural haven from early times. Bridlington was at that time two separate settlements. One mile inland from the sea was the old market town that had grown up around the Priory Church and High Street area, called Bridlington. The settlement, which had grown around the harbour, was known as Bridlington Quay, where buildings only covered a small area, from today's Bridge Street across to Beck Hill down Chapel Street to Cliff Street. The harbour was only a third of today's size. The South Pier was built in the same position as today's Chicken Run, running east from Langdales Wharf. The North Pier ran south, just outside the present position of today's North Pier. Both piers were built of wood infilled with stone. The area to the north and south of the harbour was formed by low clay cliffs, very susceptible to erosion and damage during easterly storms, as were the wooden-built piers. As late as 18 February 1836 great damage was done to the North Pier and two houses that stood at the landward end of the pier were washed into the sea. The cost of maintaining the harbour was considerable. A toll was placed on passing ships carrying coal, as well as those ships that used the harbour; the money generated was used for the constant repair of the piers and harbour structure.

The harbour was described some years later in the *Bridlington and Quay Directory* thus:

> The port though small is clean and secure but the access, owing to the narrowness of the entrance is somewhat difficult. The harbour is defended against the approach of an enemy by two batteries, one on the north side, at the end of what today is Regent Terrace, the other a little south of today's Langdale's wharf, the guns providing crossfire to protect the harbour entrance.

The effectiveness or how well equipped the forts were is open to debate. The customs officer in September 1778 sent an urgent message to Hull:

> At 7:30am. This morning, the 16th September, a small French cutter has taken four or five small ships, two or three guns from the fort fired at the privateer who moved off towards Flamborough Head. One of the smuggling cutters in the harbour has supplied the fort with

2. Bridlington Harbour 1817, showing the wooden piers and sailing ships and also the crane at Crane Wharf.

some gun powder. There is no gun powder to be got for the fort guns, – two barrels of gun powder is needed most urgently.

This was the port of Bridlington Quay when the first lifeboat arrived early in the year 1805. The shipping that travel along the coast, as well as constant battles against the elements, had a secondary danger to contend with, that of French warships patrolling the North Sea capturing or sinking any English shipping they came across, as England had been at war with France since 1793. These dangers are described in a Hull newspaper on 21 January 1805:

> On Friday night arrived at Leith, the *Swallow*, Captain White from London. On Wednesday morning, being off Flamborough Head, a French brig privateer came close upon her stern, through a fleet of colliers, and was within pistol shot, before Captain White knew she was an enemy, and saw her loading her guns. The Frenchman calls out repeatedly to 'Haul To'. Captain White, ordering down his square sail and immediately cleared his deck to engage. In the meantime the Frenchman hauled his colours halfway up his mainsail, and fired a broadside with a volley of musketry: but being opposed, with as much precision and regularity as the suddenness of the alarm admitted, with round and grapeshot from the smacks 12 pound Carronades, he, after a short time, thought it proper to steer off to a safe distance, keeping up his fire, but without doing any injury. After some time, an English ship came down upon the privateer, and hastened their retreat. She kept hovering about however all-day, and it is feared may have taken several vessels in the evening. Captain White fought with the greatest resolution and we are happy to say neither ship nor crew sustained any damage. As this short engagement was quite close to Flamborough Head it is regretted there was not a battery upon it, as a few guns might not only protect the whole fleet but would have blown this privateer to the bottom. She was a black-sided Brig, mounting apparently 14 guns.

Despite all the problems of the time the lifeboat was now established at Bridlington Quay. Unfortunately no records remain of the early lifeboat; we have to rely on a few small newspaper entries that survive.

During the early development of the lifeboat, men were looking at other ways to prevent shipwrecks. One idea was to position lighthouses to shine lights out across the sea to the masters of ships moving along the coast to show or mark positions of cliffs or points of danger. Each lighthouse had a different light or set of lights. The masters were then able to segregate each cliff or landmass from the next along the coast during the hours of darkness.

An application to build one such lighthouse on Flamborough headland was put forward on 21 January 1805:

> The plan for a lighthouse, intended to be erected on Flamborough head, is now invented on a very peculiar construction, and submitted to the inspection of Trinity house, ship owners underwriters and merchants of London, Hull, Newcastle and other ports.
>
> We believe that it meets with the general approbation of all that are concerned in the preservation of property and the lives of mariners at sea and that it will be carried into effect. The plan is the invention of Benjamin Milne, Esq. Collector of his Majesty's customs at the port of Bridlington. It is to be constructed with two lights revolving on a horizontal plane, 70 feet from the ground, reflected by concave mirrors, appearing to the mariner at sea alternatively 70 feet asunder, and then as one light by eclipsing each other as they pass round every five minutes, by which means they will be distinguishable from all other lighthouses on the coast. These most perilous rocks at Flamborough head, on which loss of property, and the scene of great distress, occur, may then be passed with safety.

The Bridlington Quay lifeboat must have been kept, without doubt, on or close to the harbour side. One important factor was the need for the boat to be transported on a transporting carriage, to the site of the wreck, which frequently took place some distance from the harbour, at any point along the coastline. In Bridlington's case this also included the fact that the harbour is and always has been tidal. If the boat was to be available 24 hours a day, it had to be transported across the beach at low water then launched into the open sea. The boat was backed into the surf with enough depth of water that the boat might be launched from the carriage, with the crew seated and ready to pull on the oars, its keel resting on rollers; comparatively little force was required to launch. Such force was applied by means of ropes attached to the stern passing through pulleys at the outer end of the carriage, so that people on shore could haul the ropes inland in order to force the boat off its carriage seaward.

The First Lifeboat House

It appears that the lifeboat was kept in the open until an application was sent to the Lords Feoffees, who owned a building used by the Harbour Master, after which a public meeting was held, by the Harbour Commissioners, at the *Ship Inn* Bridlington Quay, pursuant to a public advertisement, 17 September 1805:

> The Committee for managing the concerns, relative to the lifeboat at this port. 'Having petitioned to have the use of the Pier House, situated on the north side of North Back Street [now Chapel Street] in Bridlington Quay, in order there in to deposit the said boat and the articles appertaining there to the said committee, undertaking to first build another house in the Clough Hole, near the bridge, of equal dimensions with the present Pier House to be occupied by their Harbour Master for the deposit there in of the Pier materials.
>
> It is ordered that the Prayer of the said petitioned shall be granted upon the terms requested: and also upon commendations that the said house shall not be used for any purpose other than for the therein depositing of the said boat and the articles to it belonging and to be at any time here after resumed by the Commissioners for the said Pier, in case the same shall be appropriated to any other use or purpose than that for which the loan there – of is now agreed.

From this agreement came the first lifeboat house.

The Pier House was situated on the corner of North Back Street (now Chapel Street) and Moor Lane (now the Promenade); today the site is occupied by the jewellers H. Samuels. From that position it was available to be taken on its carriage through the town and along the coast to the north or south if any ship was wrecked, or down Spring Pump Hill to be launched into the harbour if needed.

The following year, 1806, Flamborough Lighthouse was built by Mr John Matson of Bridlington, without the use of scaffolding. The tower was 89 ft high, standing 214ft above sea level, and the light was oil burning, with a candlepower of 13,860. Within two years the area around the port of Bridlington Quay had, at that time, two of the most important aides to maritime safety; the lighthouse on top of the cliffs at Flamborough and the Bridlington Quay lifeboat, which was ready for use 24 hours a day 365 days per year.

1808 saw a meeting of merchants and ship owners calling for a larger harbour to be built. These men and others from ports along the coast had for years joined together to buy and run sailing ships as businesses. Bridlington Quay men James Stephenson, John Clark and William Walmsley were registered in 1809 as jointly owning the *Sark*. She was used for the shipping of coal from the Tyne.

On a voyage to Bridlington Quay with a cargo of coal in December 1815, her captain, Robert Thompson, failed to navigate her into the harbour, due to the stress of weather. She became a total wreck. The fate of her crew was not recorded.

The Harbour Commissioners drew up plans for the reconstruction of the old wooden harbour. Work began in 1816; after much delay the new North Pier was completed in 1843, costing £80,000. The stone being shipped from Whitby, the South Pier took only five years to build. The harbour had been extended to the south of the old harbour, and was about three times larger than the original. It was completed in 1848, a credit to its builders. With only a minor extension to the end of the North Pier in 1866, it has withstood the savage pounding of the North Sea ever since.

Shipwrecks, together with loss of life, were so much part of coastal life, around the United Kingdom, that in 1822 Acts of Parliament were passed in order to deal with the problems that this caused:

> All vessels and goods whatsoever which came ashore without the owner or any person having them in charge, accompanying them, are wrecks, otherwise they are stranded vessels.
>
> All wrecks as soon as they take the ground, whether it be above the low water mark or within the bed of the sea, so as a man on horseback with a spear may touch the wrecks, fall into the jurisdiction of the Lord of the Manor and his bailiffs.
>
> The Church Wardens and Overseers of the poor of any parish, in which any dead human body shall be cast ashore, shall on notice thereof caused the same to be removed and with all convenient speed to be decently interred in the churchyard of burial ground of such parish. The Minister, Parish Clark and Sexton, shall perform their respective duties in the like manner, as is customary in other funerals.
>
> Any person finding such body or bodies cast ashore, and giving notice to one of the Church Wardens within six hours, shall have a reward of five shillings to be paid on demand.
>
> All costs and payments incurred by the execution of this act. Shall be paid for by the Church Wardens and Overseers. The Treasurer of such County or Riding shall then repay such sums to the said Church Warden or Overseer of the said parish.

Goods from shipwrecks were also dealt with under the Acts of Parliament of 1822.

> All persons finding or discovering upon the coast any such fine liquors or tobacco, shall, within 24 hours after such findings, giving notice to the nearest customs house or excise officer specifying the place where such goods are deposited. This only deals with spirits and tobacco no mention of lesser cargoes which did not attract such a high custom import duties to be paid to the crown.
>
> All wrecks may be claimed by the owners, within a year and a day from the time they are wrecked.
>
> A reward of a reasonable manner, according to circumstances, may be paid to all persons who inform of wrecks, or assist in securing them.

This included lifeboat crews.

The small port of Bridlington Quay in 1823 was registered as having three ship builders, two sail makers, one block and mast maker and two ropers, one of whom had been established in 1789.

The Birth of the Royal National Institution for the Preservation of Life from Shipwreck

A Yorkshireman born in 1771, Lt Colonel Sir William Hillary, a very patriotic and Christian man, had witnessed first-hand a series of wrecks on the coastline of the Isle of Man, where he resided in 1822. On seeing the tragic spectacle of seamen clinging to the rigging of vessels, then being swept into the sea to perish, he with others put out into the sea trying to save them. They used small boats that were not fit for the task. He played a leading part in the rescuing of 84 lives that year. The following year, 1823, he made an 'Appeal to the Nation' for the preservation of lives from shipwreck. It outlined the need for saving lives and how to carry out the work. He had great foresight combined with sound judgement and his main points were:

(1) The preservation of life from shipwreck
(2) Assistance to vessels in distress
(3) The preservation of vessels and property
(4) The subjects of all nations and religions in peace or war would be the equal object of the institution to rescue and help
(5) Medallions or monetary rewards be given to those who rescue lives in case of shipwreck
(6) Provision for destitute widows and families of those who lose their lives in such work.

He also looked at an umbrella structure radiating out from one main Committee of Management, overseeing branches of the institution at each lifeboat stationed around the coast. Funding for such an institution he thought would come in the form of donations from the rich and famous and also from the British public. As a result of Hillary's appeal a meeting of Noblemen and Gentlemen was called on 12 February 1824 at the *City of London Tavern*. The meeting agreed to form a National Institution. The first general meeting was held on 4 March 1824 and His Majesty King George IV agreed to become the Patron. Many others in the royal family agreed to be vice-patrons with the Prime Minister, the Earl of Liverpool, becoming the first President. Many other personalities attended the meeting, including William Wilberforce, MP for Hull, the anti-slave trade campaigner, and His Grace the Archbishop of Canterbury, who presided and moved the first resolution to form the National Institution for the Preservation of Life from Shipwreck. Later at the meeting William Wilberforce MP 'moved' a resolution that medallions or pecuniary rewards should be given to those who rescued lives. In the case of shipwreck initially there were two medals, one gold, the other silver. (In 1917 the committee of management decided to institute a bronze medal so that people could be decorated for services, which though distinguished, would not earn the award of gold or silver medal, with thanks on vellum. These decorations are recognised as an emblem of a noble act, that of saving lives.)

Shortly after the formation, its committee recorded that 39 lifeboat stations did exist around the coast, all run independently. In its first year receipts, due to the 'Liberalty of the Public', reached £9,826 6s. 6d., which enabled 12 new lifeboats to be ordered and built for the institution in 1824.

The Lloyds agent of Bridlington at this time was trying to get the local people to allow the Institution for the Preservation of Life from Shipwreck to take over the Bridlington lifeboat. At a meeting of the Institution on 11 August 1824, a letter was read from Mr Thomas Lamplough, who was a ship owner and merchant as well as agent to Lloyds at Bridlington Quay. The letter, dated 3 August 1824, stated that he had applied to the magistrates and gentlemen in that vicinity to promote the views of the Institution, but without success and saying that the lifeboat they had was much damaged as to be rendered useless and that she was too large. It would be of great service if they could get her replaced by a boat on the airtight (with air boxes fitted) principle, on a smaller scale, about 28 ft long which with oars would cost about £84 as he has been quoted from Mr Skelton of Scarborough. The secretary was directed to inform Mr Lamplough that his application would be considered.

> 13th of August 1824, The committee are of the opinion that the most pressing necessity exists for the establishment of lifeboats at the following places in England, Dover, New Haven, Brighton, Penzance and Bridlington Quay.
>
> 18th August 1824, A Letter be sent to Mr Lamplough of Bridlington Quay to say 'That in compliance with the application made to the committee in the letter of the 3rd instant they had decided on approving £84, the sum he mentions, to have a lifeboat built on the airtight principle 28 ft long by Mr Skelton of Scarborough. With a set of ash oars, which he is therefore at liberty to contract for, at that price, but that if a carriage is necessary they hope subscriptions would be raised at Bridlington Quay at that vicinity to defray the expense of it.'

To help fund the new lifeboat a letter was sent from Mr George Moor to the Hull Corporation. At their meeting of 7 December 1824 the bench resolved to grant 10 Guineas towards the Bridlington lifeboat under the condition that it was not used for the preservation of cargoes. Only that of life.

The lifeboat was subsequently built by John Skelton, a well-known boat builder of Sandside Scarborough, to the Greathead design, and placed at Bridlington Quay, replacing the Henry Greathead boat which was re-stationed at Saltfleet 1827-29 and then on the Lincolnshire coast at Donna Nook 1829-30. The Bridlington Quay lifeboat station committee accepted the new boat, with the station continuing to be independently managed. It did not come under the management of the newly formed Royal National Institution for the Preservation of Life from Shipwreck, but appears to have been interwoven with all its ideas and developments. The first annual report of the Society on 10 March 1825 shows that the Bridlington Quay Lifeboat station had become affiliated.

> The committee are happy to state that local associations, which have affiliated themselves with the institution have been formed at the following places, Dover, Brighton, Penzance, Newcastle upon Tyne and Bridlington Quay. The letters from various parts of the coast, in which an opportunity has hitherto presented itself to the committee, of granting rewards for the rescue of shipwrecked persons. It contains the most gratifying assurances that, the object of those rewards has been effectively attained and afforded. As the committee conceived the best answer to the objections, which has been urged against this institution, as embracing too large a sphere of action, but had those who urged such objections, read the rules by which the institution was governed, they would have been satisfied that the intention is to afford assistance where it is most immediately wanted and to undertake nothing beyond that power.

The criticism seems to have been against the Institution expanding, helping stations they did not have direct management of, or awarding medals and monetary awards to those same stations for deeds of outstanding bravery in saving life.

The setting up of the lifeboat service on a wave of support from public figures was very novel to the public. Such an institution was unique, unknown anywhere else in the world. Communications and the spreading of news were still only in the early stages of infancy; this fact is easily forgotten in today's world, with worldwide media coverage 24 hours a day. Most of the population lived away from the coast with little maritime interest or knowledge. The country was in a period of unrest, anxiety and distress. For some years there had been war with France bringing the fear of invasion, war against America, with hostile squadrons captained by people such as John Paul Jones patrolling our coastal waters, industrial unrest at home, the Luddites' revolt, national credit crisis with 60 banks collapsing, and widespread cholera epidemics.

The Bridlington Quay lifeboat carried out much good work. The *East Riding Gazette* of that period stated, 'the vessel sacred to humanity has become an indispensable requisite, the beneficial effects of which are experienced every season'. In line with the meeting on 4 March 1824, the Royal National Institution for the Preservation of Life from Shipwreck looked at all acts of life-saving. As do the RNLI today, awarding medals and certificates to those who save life, even though the act may not be in a lifeboat managed by them.

One of the few remaining documents about the early lifeboat is the Accounts for 1850 and 1851.

The Bridlington Lifeboat Committee in account with H. Marshall Treasurer

1850	Dr.	£	s	d
April 6th	To rope barking 9s. Postage 1s. 3d.	0	10	3
July 17th	To Labour and Horses, to get the boat cleaned and ready for painting.	1	0	3
Sept 20th	To painter, roper, as bills.	11	6	10
Nov 1st	To Gig hire and expenses, for collecting at Hunmanby, Hunmanby Moor, Filey, Thorpe, Sigglesthorne Hornsea, Driffield, Birdsal, Wold Newton	3	11	6
	Balance carried down	51	9	7
		£67	18	5

1850	Cr.	£	s	d
Mar 27th	By balance in the hands of the Treasurer as published	44	1	5
April 6th	Old rope	0	3	0
Aug. 6th	James Walker, Esq. Donation	1	0	0
Sept. 20th	Donations collected to this day	6	14	6
Oct. 16th	Donations collected to this day	11	0	6
Oct. 17th	Old cable	0	4	0
Nov. 1st	W. Jarratt, Donations collected to this day	4	15	0
		£67	18	5

1851	Dr.	£	s	d
Jan. 8th	To H. Marshall as bill	0	6	10
Jan 22nd	Expenses collecting at Hull, Driffield, Nafferton, & c.	1	6	0
Jan 22nd	To sundries to Life Boat House	0	9	6
Jan 22nd	5 Men their Yearly salaries of 10s each	2	10	0

Jan 22nd	John Hineson Boat Keeper, Yearly salary	1	1	0
Jan 22nd	Robert Scrivener collecting	0	15	0
Jan 22nd	Printer	1	9	0
Jan 28th	Sundries to Boat and House	0	5	5
Jan 27th	T and R. Lauder, for going in their Yawls to the rescue of the crew of a Schooner off Hornsea, but taken off by the crew of another Schooner before they got to them.	12	0	0
1852				
Jan 1st	Balance in the hands of the Treasurer	£78	5	1

1851	**Cr.**	**£**	**s**	**d**
Jan 1st	By balance brought down	51	9	7
Jan 22nd	Donations collected to this day	6	12	0
Jan 22nd	Annual Subscriptions of £1 and above	6	0	0
Jan 22nd	Annual Subscriptions of 10 shillings and above	4	10	0
Jan 22nd	Annual Subscriptions of 5 shillings and above	1	4	6
Jan 22nd	Annual Subscriptions of 2 shillings 6d and above	1	17	6
Jan 22nd	Annual Subscriptions of 1 shillings and above	0	6	6
	Robert Scrivener, collected from stranger vessels	5	0	0
	1 Years interest	1	5	0
		£78	5	1

Examined and found correct,
I.I. FOORD. Lient. R.N.

These Accounts show us some interesting facts: the horses used to pull the lifeboat carriage were paid for by the committee, five men had a yearly salary, John Hineson was the boat keeper (was he the equivalent of today's Lifeboat Mechanic?), people went out in gigs (a small cart pulled by a horse) to hold collections in villages all across the East Riding of Yorkshire even as far as the port of Hull, an annual subscription was paid by many people, stranger vessels (ships visiting this port for the first time?) gave donations – all for the upkeep and running of the Bridlington Quay lifeboat which was still independently run here in Bridlington. The accounts also show the lifeboat committee funding other acts of attempted life saving, by the payment made to T. and R. Lauder on 27 January 1851.

The Difficult Early Years of the National Institution for the Preservation of Life from Shipwreck

During the first 25 years of its life the National Institution struggled to survive. The country was once again going through a period of industrial unrest, as well as rebellion in Canada in 1839, the following year war with China, war in Afghanistan 1841–43, and famine in Ireland two years later. The direct result was a drop in income for the Institution, which relied heavily on voluntary contributions for its survival.

Donations and subscriptions in 1837–38 fell as low as £254, totally inadequate to meet the needs of the service at this early stage of its development.

Once again, it was a lifeboat disaster that helped to turn the tide of the public's awareness of the work the National Institution was carrying out. On 4 December 1849 the lifeboat from South Shields manned by 24 men launched to the aid of the

Betsy of Littlehampton, which had been driven on shore by a heavy easterly gale. In attempting the rescue the lifeboat capsized and only four of the crew survived. This tragedy aroused much public sympathy, which led to a revival in public attention to the sadly neglected work of the lifeboat service. On this new wave of enthusiasm, over the next few years the National Institution was reorganised. In 1851 Algernon, Duke of Northumberland, known as the Sailor Duke, accepted the vacant position as the Institute's President; he had entered the Royal Navy in 1805. One of the first things he undertook was to offer a 100-guinea prize for the best design for a lifeboat, which managed to overcome the difficulties of the present lifeboats:

(1)   They do not freely right themselves in the event of being capsized.
(2)   They are to heavy to be transported and launched along the coast when needed at the sight of a wreck.
(3)   They do not free themselves of water fast enough.
(4)   They are very expensive.

No fewer than 280 models and drawings were sent in. The various models were in the shape of catamarans, rafts, North Country cobles and ordinary boats, slightly modified.

One of the entries submitted was by Bridlington boat-builder John Ainsworth, who lived with his wife Elizabeth at 3 Cliff Street, Bridlington Quay. His boat was like a whaleboat, with a flat floor/deck, sides round in a fore and aft direction, raking stem and sternpost, clinker built of wooden planking and copper fastened. Length 34 feet, keel 26 feet, depth 4.5 feet, it had seven thwarts (seats), was pulled by 12 oars, had cork fendering and air boxes for self-righting if it overturned. The committee said it would pull well if the sea was calm. But its height out of the water in a strong wind would slow it down. If water was taken on board, from the waves, it would endanger her stability, rendering the boat liable to be upset in bad weather. This entry was unsuccessful.

After six months' examination, the prize was awarded to James Beeching of Great Yarmouth. This was the first time a boat had been designed and built specifically to be used as a lifeboat. Earlier boats by De Bernieres, Lukin, Bremner and Wouldhaves had been looked at as unsinkable self-righting boats. The committee were not altogether satisfied with Mr Beeching's boat, and Mr Peake, of Her Majesty's dockyard at Woolwich, was instructed to design a boat embodying all the best features in the plans which had been sent in. This was accordingly done and his model gradually improved as time went on. This model was adopted by the Institution for all their boats.

The lifeboats built from this design came into use, measuring from 30 to 40 feet in length and eight feet in breadth. Buoyancy is obtained by air chambers at the ends and on both sides. The two large air chambers at the stem and stern, together with a heavy iron keel, make the boat self-righting; so that should she be upset she cannot remain bottom up. Between the floor (deck) and outer skin of the boat there is a space stuffed with cork and light hard wood so that, even if a hole were made in the outer covering of the boat, it would not sink. To ensure the safety of the crew, in the event of the sea's being shipped, the floor is pierced with holes into which are placed tubes and valves so arranged that the water cannot enter the boat. Should she ship any water, the valves opened and drained the water out of the boat.

The first boat to be built from this design was taken to Brighton for trials on 3 February 1852 where it was proved:

(1) That when the boat had been hauled keel up by a crane, she righted herself in five seconds.
(2) That when righted she entirely freed herself from the water in 55 seconds.
(3) That on taking the beach to heavy rollers the boat showed great buoyancy and stability, and brought her crew onshore without shipping any water.
(4) That she could carry 30 persons beside her crew.

The year of 1852 saw many periods of severe weather conditions, which must have put the lifeboat crews under great pressure:

A shipwreck occurred on Friday night, 8th January. As the Henry William of Stockton, Thomas Moorsom Master, bound for London, was on passage and crossing the Smithic Sands, to the east of Bridlington Bay, being deeply laden with coal she struck and began to make considerable quantity of water, at the same time a heavy gale of wind was blowing, the captain decided that making for the Harbour was the best way of saving the boat and crew. But finding that it was low water decided the beach was the only alternative. With six feet of water in the hold, she grounded about quarter of mile north of the harbour, about 12 mid-night. The vessel was soon discovered by the preventive boat men who were on watch, along the foreshores, they alarmed the inhabitants of the Quay, who in a few minutes mustered in such numbers, as to be able to man the Lifeboat and put to sea by which means the whole crew were rescued from their perilous position.

The vessel has become a total wreck and the cargo (though at a loss to the underwriters) has been distributed among a considerable number of the poor on the beach by the breaking up of the vessel.

During its use in 1852 the lifeboat had suffered damage of some kind. The financial well-being of the lifeboat station must have been very fragile.

A letter dated 28 August 1852 was sent by Captain Metcalfe of Bridlington Quay to the National Institution for the Preservation of Life from Shipwreck. The letter requested £20 to pay for the repairs to the lifeboat placed at the Bridlington Quay station in 1824. The committee meeting in London on 11 November 1852 heard that Captain Washington from the RNLI had visited the station and agreed that the lifeboat had been 'Thoroughly repaired and was in good order'. The committee therefore agreed to pay £20 to Captain Metcalfe, and that 'he be thanked for his laudable exertions in getting the lifeboat put into order'.

On Wednesday night Friday 5 November 1852 Bridlington Quay was visited with one of the most violent storms it has experience in several years and considerable damage was done to shipping etc.

The brig Success of Whitby attempted to make the harbour for safety, having lost her anchor, three seas breaking over her, drove the ship off course, she drifted ashore and became a total wreck.

The brig Merchant of Hartlepool with general cargo on board also went ashore and is expected to break up.

A vessel the Sisters of Harwich, which had been deserted the previous night by her crew, was driven ashore at Mappleton.

A great deal of damage was done to the *Victoria* Public rooms, the building at the landward end of the North Pier, which is under the management of Mr. Wilson, by the waves dashing in eight large glass doors and deluging the place with water. The greater part of the jetty was washed away and also a great portion of the cliff. The amount of damage is very considerable.

Two weeks later on Saturday morning, 13 November 1852, The *Johns* of Scarborough, in ballast, came ashore at Sewerby Gap, about two miles northward of the Quay. The vessel had been observed entering the Bay on Friday night about 9 o'clock with signal light hoisted. At 3 a.m. on Saturday, all the crew were safely taken off the brig by lifeboat.

The Wreck of the *Omega*

The wreck of the *Omega*, 27 December 1852, became a turning point in the history of Bridlington Quay lifeboat, which, as far as the few remaining clues show, in my opinion had been managed by ship and sloop owners of Bridlington and Bridlington Quay. We must not forget they had to fund the running of the lifeboat themselves: reward the crews, pay for repairs to the boat and carriage, if either was damaged, plus the general upkeep of the boat and boat house, all from the own pockets or by public donations. This in no way exonerates them from the first duty which was and still is today to save lives.

The schooner *Omega* bound from South Shields to Lowestoft with a cargo of coal was seen south of Bridlington harbour sailing in a sinking state for the harbour. The wind was blowing a fearful gale south south-west with a tremendous sea lashing its fury on the schooner. As it was low tide, there was no possibility of her entering the harbour. Inevitably she was driven ashore, one mile south of the harbour, and the crew climbed the mast, taking to the rigging. On seeing the wreck, fishermen went immediately to the lifeboat house to launch the lifeboat. Mr Jarratt, one of the lifeboat committee, refused permission for its use. A new rule had recently been adopted by the committee which stated, 'The Bridlington Quay Lifeboat shall not be employed without the sanction of two key holding committee members, and that they shall proceed to view the condition of any ship or crew requiring assistance previous to giving consent'. On the refusal of the lifeboat's use, immediately the fishermen carried one of their own cobles down to the beach and launched it. The hurricane was so intense they were driven ashore, unable to reach the stricken vessel. The lifeboat was eventually launched one hour later, but was unable to provide any help. Unfortunately due to the one-hour delay caused in launching the lifeboat, the vessel had been swamped from stem to stern with tremendous breakers, becoming a total wreck, the crew were lost into the raging sea. The three crews bodies were found the next day on the rocks at Flamborough. A coroner's inquest was held; the verdict on the crew of the *Omega* was that they were found drowned.

There was a call from the fishermen for the lifeboat to be employed in bad weather to render assistance to passing sailing vessels or bring them into the harbour, if it was too dangerous for a coble to be used for this work. Was this the explanation: that the fishermen had possibly used the lifeboat as a pilot boat? After this piloting work the lifeboat had not been returned to the lifeboat boathouse and was left in a poor condition, not ready for immediate use if needed in the event of a shipwreck, the committee wanting it only to be used in cases of lifesaving? Was this the explanation for the new ruling that had been introduced to lock the boathouse doors?

In any event the tragic shipwreck of the *Omega* caused outrage in the town, with calls for the committee to resign. The outcome was a meeting at the *Britannia Hotel*, Bridlington Quay, on 10 February 1853, for the purpose of forming a committee of management, and making arrangements to secure the efficient working of the Bridlington Lifeboat, in connection with the Royal National Shipwreck Institutions it was attended by Captain J. R. Ward, the Inspector of Lifeboats for the National Shipwreck Institution, who had come down from London for the purpose of reorganising measures for the efficient management of the boat. (The former Committee had resigned their charge to the Institution.) All the principal seamen and fishermen at the Port of Bridlington Quay asked Thomas Prickett, Esq. to take the chair, who explained to the Meeting the object of their having been convened.

> Captain Ward, RN acquainted the meeting with the object and wishes of the National Shipwreck Institutions, regarding the management of their boats, and their desire to afford every facility and advantage to the crews who would have to risk their lives in them. The Lifeboat Regulations of the National Shipwreck Institutions were then read to the seamen present, who were particularly requested to state any objections, which they might entertain towards any portion of them, and after full explanations and discussions, they were unanimously agreed to with the exception of a few immaterial particulars, which were considered inapplicable to this locality.

Among other arrangements, it was resolved that two old sailors were to be appointed boat keepers, to be held answerable for the boat and everything connected with her being kept in proper order and ready for service, under the superintendence of the chief captain; the boat keepers to receive £4 per annum jointly.

The following gentlemen were elected a committee (with power to add to their number); to have the future management of the lifeboat, subject to the rules as amended of the Royal National Institution for the Preservation of Life from Shipwreck.

Rev. Francis Simpson (Chairman)	Mr Stephenson
Arthur Strickland Esq.	Mr John Allison
Edward Harding Esq.	Mr John Fell
Captain Elliot RN	Mr G. Richardson
Dr Pearson	Mr W. Wallis
Mr W. Watson (Secretary and Treasurer)	(Chief Capt. of the Lifeboat)

On Friday 25 February 1853, a meeting of the committee was held at Bridlington Quay, at which it was resolved:

> That six keys of the lifeboat house are to be thus kept:
>   One in charge of the person who occupies the room over the lifeboat house;
>   One with the two old sailors appointed to take care of the boat,
>   One with the chief captain, who takes command of the boat when at sea;
>   One with the Secretary;
> The remaining keys always to be kept with some members of the committee residing in Bridlington Quay and at present are kept by A. Strickland Esq. and E. Harding Esq.

Any one person in charge of a key to be fully authorised to grant the use of the boat when required, but the boat on no account to be used except in cases of a wreck or a vessel making signals of distress.

It was further resolved, that a brief statement should be printed of the measures which had been adopted for the future management of the boat, and circulated among the subscribers and general public, with an earnest appeal and requests from the committee that they would, by continuing their contributions and support, enable them to provide for the efficiency and management of the boat, which has since its inception, been the means of rescuing several persons from inevitable destruction. The Secretary, or any member of the committee will thankfully receive subscriptions. Annual subscriptions become due on the first of January.

Francis Simpson, Chairman.

The Bridlington Quay lifeboat had now become part of the Royal National Institution for the Preservation of Life from Shipwreck. On its taking over the management of the station, it was noted that the lifeboat was in a fair state of repair, being maintained by a toll of six pence on each vessel entering the harbour.

The following year, 1854, the name of the Institution was changed to the 'Royal National Life-Boat Institution'.

As a direct result of the success of James Peak's lifeboat design of 1851, numerous trials and modifications took place. The boat had been rigorously tested on the coast by the Inspector of Lifeboats during the winter period in all weathers, and was to become the design for the RNLI's self-righting fleet over the next 50 years.

The *Robert Whitworth*

In 1864 the RNLI decided to change the lifeboat at Bridlington to the *Robert Whitworth*. She had undergone her trials in the Regent Canal, London where her self-righting and water ejecting qualities were successfully demonstrated. She was 33 feet long by eight feet wide, pulling ten oars double-banked. She had been built with a hull construction of two-and-a-half-inch thickness of mahogany diagonally laid across each other for strength by Forrest of Limehouse, London. The new launching carriage was built for the boat by J. Robinson of Kentish Town, London, which had been fitted with the device enabling the boat to be launched with her crew onboard with the oars ready, to give them time to make headway into the breakers before being beaten back broadside onto the beach. This consisted of a simple pulley system. The cost of the new lifeboat and carriage amounted to £390. This sum was raised in Manchester by the efforts of Mr *Robert Whitworth* of the Manchester RNLI branch; as a result, the naming ceremony was held in the city of Manchester less than one week after the London trials. The lifeboat arrived in Manchester for the naming ceremony, which took place on 22 November 1864. Mr Robert Whitworth's wife formally named the lifeboat, breaking a bottle of wine against the lifeboat bow, saying, 'Let this lifeboat henceforth be known by the name of the *Robert Whitworth* and may she under the blessing of almighty God be the instrument of rescuing many lives from the perils of the sea'. After the naming ceremony a Grand Parade took place through the principal streets of Manchester, headed by the band of the 1st Manchester Rifle Volunteers.

It was planned that the *Robert Whitworth* would be paraded similarly in Leeds and Bradford before being delivered to Bridlington, but before the plan could be carried out, the weather intervened. During a devastating storm the Tynemouth lifeboat had been launched to assist the crew of the SS *Stanley*, which had run aground. During this rescue the Tynemouth lifeboat suffered great damage and the decision was made to divert the *Robert Whitworth* to the Tynemouth station, to deputise for the lifeboat there, until she could be repaired. She stayed at Tynemouth until Thursday, 12 January 1865 when she was transported by rail, arriving at Bridlington railway station on the Saturday evening.

At 11am on Monday 16 January, the new lifeboat *Robert Whitworth*, with her crew onboard, paraded through the streets of the town, drawn by eight horses, preceded by the band of the 5th East Yorkshire Rifle Volunteers and the 1st East Yorkshire Artillery Volunteers. After the parade, the lifeboat was taken onto the beach where she was launched to the salute of the field gun and the cheers of the assembled crowd. She was put through her paces at sea under the guidance of Capt. Robertson of the RNLI before being re-carriaged and transported to the new boathouse which had been built for her at a cost of £192 2s. 0d., on the corner of Railway Crescent (now Windsor Crescent) and Old Hilderthorpe Road (now South Cliff Road). The old boathouse had become too small and congested, being in the centre of the growing town. From the new site she was close to the slipway onto the South Pier, where she was easily launched into the harbour or taken down the slipway at the landward end of the South Pier onto the beach to be launched at the site of any wreck to the south. If she was needed to the north, the lifeboat and carriage could be pulled through the town to be launched down Trinity Cut or Sands Lane slipway.

The lifeboat coxswain was paid a retaining fee; he was responsible for the efficiency and general good order of the boathouse, the boat and her gear along with selecting the lifeboat crew, who were all volunteers. On receiving the information of a wreck

3. *The lifeboat house at the junction of Railway Crescent and South Cliff Road, 1890*

or vessel in distress the coxswain alerted the crew – by day it was by hoisting a flag and by night the firing of a carronade or other alarm signal. Almost immediately the fishermen and seamen of the town rushed to the boathouse, soon becoming a large crowd. If this happened during the day, boys from the local school would be among the crowd. They were there being able to run faster than their fathers, who may have been working on the fishing boats at the north side of the harbour or at the end of South Pier. The coxswain would open the small back door of the lifeboat house just enough to leave a small gap, through which the crowd were forced to squeeze to get into the boathouse. Along one side of the lifeboat hung a row of lifebelts and anyone who managed to grab a lifebelt became a member of the lifeboat crew. If the young boys could manage to get a belt they would duck out of sight under the lifeboat carriage, with the lifebelt, to hide for a few minutes until their fathers arrived, probably out of breath after the run from the pier, to put on the lifebelts and take their places as crew-members of the lifeboat. The lifeboat crew got a small remuneration. If lives or boats were saved this remuneration could be increased by payments from the owners of the vessels, so there was strong competition for a place in the lifeboat crew. In times of poor fishing or bad weather this was valuable money, which helped buy food for the table. Those men not able to get a lifebelt scrambled around to the other side of the lifeboat where a row of buckets stood. Possession of a bucket entitled a man to help with the launching and recovering of the lifeboat. They also received a remuneration, though much smaller than the lifeboat crew. Launching required some men to wade into the sea steering the carriage. As the horses dragged the lifeboat into the water, other men waited to make sure the lifeboat slid smoothly off the carriage into the sea; if not they waded into the surf to help. On the occasions when the horses were not available, the men would pull the lifeboat into the sea.

Lifeboats were now being built with large air cases at the bow and stern, with smaller ones positioned insdie the boat. The high bow and stern air cases combined with a heavy keel provided the Lifeboats with self-righting capabilities. The two air cases were rounded on the top. In the water the tendency is for a boat that has capsized to fall back to one side or the other, because the rounded air boxes allow the heavy keel to drag the boats back over into the correct position.

Launching the lifeboat to ships in distress or wrecks in gale-force winds, with huge breaking waves, frequently causes it to take on water. Therefore, bailing becomes necessary, but the crew cannot give their undivided attention to rowing the lifeboat while bailing out water, which makes the lifeboat less efficient. The discharge of water from a lifeboat relies on the fact that water will and must find its own level, that is no amount of water, great or small, can remain above its flat and level surface in the lowest attainable position.

The deck of the lifeboat of this time, when afloat, was above the level of water in which it floats. The space between the deck and the keel is filled with cork. Six large holes in the boat deck are fitted with six metal tubes, which pass right through the bottom of the boat's hull, making six large openings into the sea. In the six tubes are valves or flaps, which will only open downwards to let water down and out, not upwards into the boat. When a large breaking wave crashes into the boat, being above the level of the sea, it immediately seeks its own level by escaping through the tubes in the deck, back into the sea.

The lifeboat frees herself of water in less than two minutes. The buoyancy of the lifeboat is not affected for more than a few seconds by the tons of water, which frequently break over her.

During this period, questions were being asked in Parliament. On 16 February 1866 the Earl of Malmesbury called attention to what he saw as the inefficiency for the plans of saving human life on the coast of the United Kingdom. He urged the Government to take charge of this duty and provide adequate means at the public cost. He believed that the very excellent society which undertook this duty did not desire Government aid, believing it would do more harm than good, but as the country was the first maritime power, the Government ought to see that this duty was thoroughly discharged all round the coast. The Duke of Somerset paid a strong testimony to the value of the National Lifeboat Institution and was against the Government taking on the duty, which the Institution so efficiently discharged. By so doing they would destroy a noble local Institution without doing much good themselves. At the present time the Institution had more boats than they had efficient crews for, and the coastguards were most zealous in rescuing life when it could. The Rocket Apparatus brigade, which was quite different from the lifeboat service, had rescued many lives. These Brigades were entirely paid for by the Government. Lord Stanley of Alderney said the Lifeboat Institution had supplied 11 lifeboats to France. After the Emperor witnessed their efficiency he had desired to have the Society's service established on the French coast. The debate continued.

The *Harbinger* Lifeboat

After the problems of 1853 some fishermen looked for a second lifeboat to use also as a pilot boat, and a foy boat (a boat which takes water and provisions to the many boats anchored in the Bay), but they needed a benefactor. Residing in the Quay, and a friend of many fishermen, was Count Gustave Batthyany, who had fled to England after the 1849 Hungarian revolt against the Austrian Empire. His father, who had been a Hungarian Prince, had been executed.

In 1865 the RNLI had changed the lifeboat at Bridlington to the *Robert Whitworth* which was longer and heavier than the old boat. Some fishermen disagreed with its design and criticised its handling at sea.

At this time Count Batthyany agreed to fund a new boat for the fishermen, commissioning local man, David Purdon, to build the boat in his workshop, nextdoor to 32 North Street. It was to be built to the fishermen's own specifications. She was smaller than the *Robert Whitworth*, was built of mahogany, had bow and stern air cases to make her self-righting, was self-draining, and carvel built (planks laid edge to edge to form a smooth surface, as opposed to the overlapping planks of a clinker built boat). When finished she was painted a stone colour, and was to be crewed by nine men.

The boat was named the *Harbinger*. She first tasted salt water on Monday afternoon, 1 January 1866. She was launched opposite the slipway, half a mile north of Bridlington harbour, in the presence of several hundred spectators. She was then rowed into the harbour to undergo trials. Her crew intentionally capsized her and took a very cold bath; the boat righted herself to the correct position. She was then nearly filled with water by removing three of the four plugs in her deck; she emptied herself while

4. *The* Harbinger *stationed on the harbour side – covered to protect the lifeboat from the weather.*

afloat in less than half a minute. She was stationed in or near the harbour, so as to be ready for any emergency as a lifeboat, and be employed in the usual way. Should any money from a foy be earned, the boat share would go towards the upkeep of the *Harbinger*. It was said, 'Great credit is due to the builder, and she is a very smart boat and sails uncommonly well'.

On the afternoon of 10 October 1865 the brig *Sarah Horn*, of Whitstable, in ballast, Captain Loft in command, entered Bridlington Bay showing a signal for assistance, having lost her top mast and received other damage during a storm.

Whilst trying to go to their aid, a sad disaster occurred to the crew of the coble *Fly* (a full account can be seen in Medal, Vellum and Certificate Services, p.117). The lifeboat was manned and launched. On reaching the *Sarah Horn* the crew were taken off and four men from the lifeboat were left on board the brig. These men were relieved on the following morning by four other men. In the course of the day, with extra hands, the brig was safely manoeuvred into the harbour. For their services rendered in salvaging the *Sarah Horn*, the 22 men plus two shares for the lifeboat, made a claim for £150. R.D. Preston, barrister, instructed by Mr Harland, appeared in court on behalf of the men. He most ably advocated their case, endeavouring to show that for their valuable service, including time lost in fishing and labour, etc. they deserved and were fully entitled to this sum. Mr Amos, owner of the brig, pleaded his own case and contended that the charge for what had been done by the men to and for the brig was excessive and most exorbitant.

After a long and patient hearing of the pros and cons, the magistrate awarded the men the sum of £75 to share between them and the Lifeboat, plus costs.

Even when anchored in the Bay sailing ships were not safe if the wind strengthened from the east or south.

A terrific gale came suddenly from the south, on Monday 29 October 1865, and with it torrential rain. During the day a brig, *Garibaldi* of London, parted from her anchor when in the Bay, being driven ashore under Sewerby cliffs. Rockets with lines attached were fired over her by the coastguards the crew were saved. A barque, the *Frederick* of Blyth, was also driven ashore in the same place. The *Charles Little* of London, carrying a cargo of coal, went ashore south of the South Pier, after being driven from her anchor by the gale, and all her crew were saved. Two of the vessels were later brought into harbour, after the gale decreased.

During a fearful storm that swept the coast on 16 January 1866, a vessel together with its crew was lost. The ship, with a crew of five onboard carrying a cargo of coal from Seaham, sprang a leak. The captain attempted to find safety in the nearest harbour but the stress of the storm-force wind prevented this. The water in the ship's hold was rising fast and her crew were becoming increasingly exhausted by continually working at the pumps. The only way to save the ship and crew was to run the ship onto the shore. Because of the weather, the vessel had become practically unmanageable. Heavy seas had carried away the deck house together with some sails and rigging, and the pumps eventually became choked and of no use. The schooner drifted at the mercy of the elements, her crew working to clear the pumps and eventually putting them back into working order; without them she would have foundered within the hour. Four hours later the vessel was sighted close to the shore. The coastguards were immediately called out and the rocket apparatus cart was pulled down onto the beach. As the vessel came ashore the rocket brigade fired the first rocket. The vessel was laying end-on to the shore, making it extremely difficult to fire a line across the ship. The second rocket line went directly across the ship, high in the tattered rigging. Three of the crew were on the weather side and could see the means of their rescue,

5. *The model of the* Harbinger *in the Bayle Museum – note the seats, and life-lines running down the inside of the boat and also the self-bailing holes through the bottom of the boat.*

but it was out of reach due to their exhaustion. Not one of them had the strength to climb the rigging to get hold of the rocket line. The next rocket line missed the ship completely. The following rocket went across the deck, the rope landing across the shoulder of one of the crew. The man desperately clung onto the line and was dragged halfway to the shore and safety, when he lost his grip and was washed under the sea and drowned by the receding wave. The master and mate were by this time hanging onto ropes over the side of the ship, which was now laid towards the shore. The cabin boy, who was on deck, seeing his master hanging from shipside in the water, shouted, asking if he could help them. No answer was heard as the boy was immediately swept into the boiling sea by a huge breaking wave which crashed across the ship. The boy was not seen again. The same wave also washed a crewman off the deck; both perished in the short distance between the ship and the shore. The ship's small boat had been washed into the sea close to where the captain and mate were. Both men grabbed it, hanging on to its side. Their bodies were still trailing in the water and they were washed towards the shore by the breaking waves. Two coastguards, wearing cork lifebelts, waded out into the surf to help the survivors to safety. From the time the vessel struck the shore to the time she broke in two was no more than ten minutes. She had become waterlogged and unmanageable, with six inches of water above the cabin deck when she went on to the shore. Two men and one boy were lost, together with the vessel and its cargo.

The RNLI took on board the concerns of the Bridlington men with regard to the *Robert Whitworth*'s being too big and difficult to row. In 1866 they provided a new lifeboat to replace the *Robert Whitworth*, which was re-stationed at Whitehaven, where she was re-named *Elizabeth*.

The name *Robert Whitworth* was then transferred to the new lifeboat, which had been built to the same basic design, by Forrestt of Limehouse, London, at a cost of £242. She was 32 feet long, 7 feet 6 inches beam, self-righting and she weighed 2.1 tons. She was smaller than the original *Robert Whitworth*, but was built on much finer lines and proved to be more acceptable to the men for the conditions experienced in Bridlington Bay.

The *Harbinger* quickly became a popular lifeboat with the fishermen. This was possibly because she was a good sea boat, easy to handle, and there were few restrictions on her use. She did not meet the RNLI's stringent design requirements; her management was declined by the Institution. As a result the *Robert Whitworth* became known as the National Lifeboat and the *Harbinger* as the Fishermen's Lifeboat. These two lifeboats were stationed at Bridlington and were standing by on 10 February 1871, when the East Yorkshire coast was swept by a storm of great violence unequalled within the living memory of the inhabitants of Bridlington Quay.

2

The Great Gale, 10 February 1871, and its Aftermath

Flamborough Head has always been a major landmark for coastal traffic, especially for those ships sailing south. A distinct point of recognition along the coast was so important when captains had only very basic navigation aids to rely on a compass, a watch and the stars at night. Such basic navigation brought with it uncertainty of a ship's true position, which tended to make masters of sailing ships sail close to the coast to keep, where possible, in sight of land which in turn caused many ships to be wrecked.

Stretching to the south of Flamborough Head is Bridlington Bay. Referred to by seafarers as the 'Bay of Safety', when gales blow from the north or west, many ships would anchor to wait for the gale to blow itself out, or possibly for a favourable wind with which to continue their voyage. In stark contrast, when the wind blows from the east or south the Bay changed in the days of sail to a lee shore, a death trap, for the wooden ships of the coastal trade. Most were old and rotten, heavily laden with cargo, sluggish to handle at sea, and in bad weather they became floating coffins.

6. *Sailing ships moored in the harbour, late 1800s. Note the lifeboat house in the centre of the photograph.*

Henry Jackson was 17 years old when he sailed on the brig *Willow Castle*. On 19 February 1866 he wrote a letter from South Shields to his parents; part of it is as follows:

Thank God I have arrived in Shields and I am very glad, we had a bad passage down I am sorry to say that we were all nearly lost for we ran ashore on the sands, but we were very close to the rocks, if we had struck the rocks we should of all perished, but thanks be to God we did not, it was on the 1st February when it was done, there were three lifeboats came out to us [probably two lifeboats and a coble] to take us ashore, but we managed to take one of our anchors out to sea and get a long line fast to it and then pull the ship out and then we got the ship off. It was very foggy that morning it was at Bollington [slang for Bridlington] Bay near Flamborough Head there had been some fearful Gales since Sunday night. Nothing would hold the ship you would not credit it, I think the ship is going to be sold for she is severely damaged and think she is not fit to go to sea any more.

On 19 October 1869 an inhabitant of Bridlington Quay sent a letter to the editor of *The Times*:

Sir, six weeks ago a coal brig came onshore in this bay, in comparatively smooth water. About 18 hours sailing time from here she had sprung a leak, and the water overpowering the pumps, the men desperately drove her onto the sands to save their lives. The fact is she was so old and rotten that she could not hold together any longer. Accordingly the wreck with a part of the cargo was sold for £42, and then she was broken up for firewood. It appears she was built at Shields in 1828. Consequently she had been 41 years old and was uninsured. I conclude no office would be burdened with her, but her owners went on sailing her at all hazards. Now this I believed to be the history of a large proportion of our coasting vessels and colliers.

At this moment the North West wind is blowing fiercely, we have had an awful night. Six ships have come in here disabled; we shall have the usual black record of damage and destruction. I wonder how many of these old ships will meet their fate and go down with all hands. Why in the name of humanity, are vessels allowed to swim until they sink. If a vessel is too rotten to be insured surely she is unfit to go to sea; and yet these old leaky ships are the coffins in which our merchant seamen are sent to meet a watery grave. I believe that if a true account were taken, it would be found that a large proportion of the vessels annually wrecked, would have been long ago condemned as utterly unseaworthy by any government agent. Why should not inspectors or agents be appointed to decide when a ship is unsafe and if necessary have our old ships broken up.

We gladly contribute towards lifeboats, but while we are preserving life with one hand we are destroying it with the other.

I remain yours respectfully

A. O. Bridlington Quay.

In January 1871 the *Hull News* condemned the indifference of the House of Commons:

A state of things more discreditable to British legislation could hardly be conceived of than the system which allows the sacrifice of nearly 1000 lives every year through vessels being allowed to leave our ports in an unseaworthy condition. Mr Samuel Plimsoll, M.P. for Derby was fighting hard in Parliament to get markings on the ships sides. Showing the legal limit by which each ship could be submerged with the weight of cargo under various conditions safely. He was to use the events which took place the following month in Bridlington, to eventually change the system safeguarding the crews of British vessels forever.

During the Victorian age it was the vogue to refer to a storm- or hurricane-force wind as 'The Great Gale'. One such occurred on Friday, 10 February 1871, remembered at Bridlington above all the others for causing extensive destruction to lives, property and ships in the Bay; the fearful disaster was witnessed by the inhabitants of Bridlington Quay.

The previous day, Thursday 9th, had been a mild day of bright sunshine with a light favourable north-westerly wind blowing. Such weather had allowed about 400 vessels, which had been weather bound in the ports on the Tees and the Tyne, to put to sea, many with cargoes of coal for London and Paris. All went well until 3a.m. on Friday morning when the ships were off Bridlington Bay. The skies started to show evidence that the wind and weather were changing and the wind strengthened and veered to the south-east. Suddenly a storm hit the fleet, rapidly increasing to a hurricane, which was accompanied with blinding sleet and snow. The ships were now on a lee shore; by 6 a.m. in the morning the wind was blowing from the east-south-east.

Crowds had started to gather, but the storm-force wind and blinding snow made it difficult to see far to seaward. About 7a.m. the two lifeboats and rocket apparatus were all prepared in anticipation of the impending emergency. High tide was at 7.10 a.m. With the strengthening ebb tide running against the wind, the sea state would deteriorate.

The first vessel to be seen in distress was *Friends Increase* of London, a south-country barge making for the safety of the harbour, which she failed to make, hitting the sea wall in front of the Esplanade. The crew took to the rigging, as the violent sea crashed over them, and five coastguards tried with the rocket apparatus to reach them without success. The *Robert Whitworth* lifeboat was launched, and Coxswain James Stephenson in command managed to get alongside, bringing the crew ashore to safety. By this time more ships could be seen, all at the mercy of the weather. The captains had three choices; the first was to try to make the harbour, through the confused sea, with a ship that was difficult to handle. This choice no longer existed after 9.30a.m. as the tide ebbed. The second choice was to run the ship ashore in the hope that the crew could then make the dry land and safety through the boiling surf. The third option was to anchor in the Bay and hope to ride out the storm. As the vessels were old and rotten with poor gear, it was highly unlikely that their anchors and cables would stand any chance of holding the vessels to seaward in such weather.

At about ten o'clock, vessel after vessel, powerless against the wind, was driven onshore. The crews were in perishing conditions, the snow falling heavily at intervals only broken by rain and sleet. Three schooners and two brigs, all carrying cargoes of coal, came ashore near the sea wall and immediately started to break up from a pounding of the heavy surf. The *Robert Whitworth* was re-launched with the help of those on the beach. The *Harbinger*, due to the ebbing tide at 11 a.m., was unable to get out of the harbour to continue her valiant work of saving life. Fishermen, together with onlookers, pulled her from the harbour and carried the lifeboat on their shoulders over a mile to the slipway onto the North Beach to launch her.

As a crew man in either boat became exhausted, or unable to carry on due to bleeding hands from rowing, without hesitation a volunteer took his place. Both lifeboat crews, rocket apparatus brigade and coastguards were at full stretch. All were helped by the unsung heroes, the townspeople, many of whom were taking into their houses

7. *The* Robert
Whitworth *lifeboat 1871.*

those who had been rescued, giving them warm clothes, food and hot drinks, others
helping to land then re-launch the lifeboats by hand or helping with rescues along the
shoreline. A smack belonging to Colchester was stranded at Sewerby; being small she
went well up the beach, and her crew managed to walk ashore as the tide ebbed. Near
to her, a brig loaded with coal, on striking the rock scar, had knocked her bottom
out, losing her cargo. She was pushed up the beach by the heavy breaking swell. The
crew launched their small boat in the hope of reaching the shore and coastguards on
the beach waded into the water pulling the drowning man in the swamped boat to
the safety of dry land. The *Robert Whitworth* saved six crew from the brigantine *Echo*,
re-launching to rescue six from the Lynn brig, *Windsor*, followed by the saving of
crews from two or three other vessels, accounts vary. The *Harbinger* saved the crew of
six from the North Shields brig, *Agility*, before re-launching to rescue the four crew
of the Shields schooner, *Bebside*.

The crew of the *Robert Whitworth* during the morning had become exhausted while
rowing their institution boat, carrying out the work in shallow waters. On returning
to the beach from the last rescue both lifeboat man and rescue crew had to be lifted
out of the lifeboat, exhausted. The conditions had become too bad for the RNLI
boat to continue; she was taken out of service, after saving 16 lives.

As the *Harbinger* continued the good work, boats were still being driven ashore. A
coal-laden brig was driven onto the beach by the raging storm 120 yards from the
North Pier. The crew climbed into the rigging, the rocket apparatus made contact but
the crew were too cold and exhausted to help themselves, falling from the rigging
into the water and drowning. One or two boats attempted to get into the harbour,
but because of low water they were swept past the entrance and driven against the
pier walls. A collier brig attempted the same; she, like the schooner, struck the beach,
and started to break up as her timbers were rotten; the crew perished. About the
same time the schooner *Produce* of Folkestone was wrecked near the sea wall within
shouting distance of the shore. Despite efforts by the rocket apparatus team, four of
the crew perished, and two other crew-members tried to launch their ship's own
small boat, which capsized, tossing them into the sea. The remaining two crewmen
attempted to swim ashore; one was lost beneath the waves almost immediately. The

second, a strong swimmer, received much encouragement from the crowd along the pier. He had his leg crushed by a large piece of timber from one of the wrecks, just before reaching the safety of the North Pier; he too sank beneath the waves, in full view of those who had given him encouragement.

Near the same place a collier sank, and the crew took to the small ship's boat, which capsized in the horrendous seas around it. One man was pulled out of the water alive but died soon after.

The *Harbinger* lifeboat crew took her out time and time again and as one of the oarsmen became exhausted another took his place; a brig, a schooner, the *Squirrel* fishing boat, another collier – all the crews were rescued by the small *Harbinger* lifeboat.

The *Vivid*, Captain Vary in command, had sailed from Scarborough on Thursday afternoon. In attempting to enter Bridlington harbour, she drifted to the south, and ran ashore. The lifeboat managed to save all the crew.

Shortly afterwards the Whitby brig *William Maitland* went aground near Ulrome, south of Bridlington. The captain tried to persuade his crew to get into the water, using anything that would float, in the hope that they would be washed ashore to safety. The crew, petrified, decided to stay on board. The captain after doing all he could to persuade his crew to follow him, jumped overboard and reached the shore safely. The crew had taken to the rigging as heavy seas were constantly pounding the ship. At about 6.30 p.m. a huge wave took the mast away, sweeping the crew to their deaths.

A three-masted vessel was seen to disappear near Flamborough Head, another ship to the south sank with all hands, two others were driven ashore at Auburn, resulting in the loss of nine men, and so the devastation continued.

The crew members of the *Harbinger*, as they became exhausted, were replaced by volunteers. After the seventh time she returned with survivors to the beach, one poor fellow was so exhausted that it was feared he would die; however, he was taken safely home. His place was taken by David Purdon, the builder of the lifeboat. A second crew member was replaced by John Clappison, David Purdon's assistant. The *Harbinger* was then launched to a brig, which was stranded on the South Beach. The lifeboat crew managed to land the five shivering survivors to the applause and cheers of the people waiting to help on the beach. The brig *Delta* of Whitby was ashore to the south of the harbour. The *Harbinger* was manhandled once again back into the surf and re-launched. She could be seen from the harbour, rising on the crest of the waves, and then sinking down into the trough and out of sight, again and again. The *Harbinger* crew struggled through the treacherous seas to reach the *Delta*. During this time, four of the brig's crew had launched the ship's small boat, in an attempt to reach the shore, but had been swamped by a huge wave and all were drowned. As the *Harbinger* came up to the stern of the *Delta*, one old crewman was seen to be holding on to the rigging of the vessel. The flowing tide and the howling storm combined to produce a heavy breaking sea at the wreck of the *Delta*. Due to the heavy sea that was running, Coxswain Robinson had to decide when to move alongside the *Delta*, to take the man off. A huge wave lifted her upwards close to the wreck. Coxswain Robinson shouted to the man, 'After the next wave has passed, jump into the lifeboat'; whether the man was too afraid or unable to jump will never be known. A large wave crashed against the stranded vessel and then surged back at the lifeboat, forcing her

8. Painting of the Great Gale, 1871.

stern low into the water. The next wave followed almost immediately. It was massive, striking the little *Harbinger* with terrific force, and she was forced up into the air before being driven upside down into the boiling sea. The brave crew, who had risked so much to save the lives of others that day, were in an instant struggling for their own. In the confusion that followed the *Harbinger* floated keel upwards for two or three minutes; Hopper managed to climb on to the upturned hull. He helped Pickering get hold of the boat but then Pickering lost his grip and was washed away by the breaking waves. Hopper then offered a hand to Watson. Before he could grasp the hand, the sea washed him away from the boat. Hopper pulled off his scarf and held it out to Robinson, who managed to get hold of it before tying it on to the side of the boat. Shortly after this the boat righted itself. Due to the boat's motion, Robinson was thrown into the boat, to find Richard Bedlington, who had been underneath the boat's hull all the time and had been listening to Hopper and Robinson talking. They both helped Hopper get into the boat. As a result of the capsized lifeboat, all the contents of the boat, including oars, had been lost or broken, leaving the lifeboat and three survivors at the mercy of the sea. The boat was washed on to the beach, badly damaged, near Wilsthorpe. Bedlington, Hopper and Robinson were helped ashore by Mr Robert Dobson and taken to the home of Mr Appleby in Wilsthorpe, where they were cared for. Only a few hours after the *Harbinger* capsized the sea gave up the body of David Purdon, washing it ashore.

The *Harbinger* had suffered too much damage to be of any further use that day, and it was impossible to launch the *Robert Whitworth* due to the sea conditions. But still the work went on, men on the piers, sea wall and beach endeavouring to save life. Several other vessels were being blown ashore as the tide flowed. Ships from the fleet that had sailed innocently south only 30 hours ago were now being driven ashore at the mercy of the weather. Their crews could be clearly seen on the deck and in the rigging. The rocket apparatus was brought and several shots were fired without any luck, the sea frequently breaking over the vessels. As the tide rose, the vessels began to rock violently with the motion of the sea, the wrecks becoming match wood. Their were crews perishing in the storm-tossed sea.

Flamborough fishermen had gathered, watching the events from south of the Head. The brig *Arrow* of Sunderland was driven ashore nearby. The local rocket life-saving company managed to save two crewmen, before the vessel started to break up. The fishermen ran to South Landing and carried a coble on their shoulders to where the brig was, and launched the coble. They rowed off to the *Arrow*. Leonard Mainprize managed to climb on board, where he found a seaman tangled in a mass of rope, almost unconscious. Leonard cut the man free and then with the help of the other fishermen lifted him into the coble and rowed ashore safely.

The destructive work of the storm and the loss of human life was not yet finished. After dark a man was seen clinging to the mast of a schooner, aground near the pier. In his hand a light, as a signal for help from those on the shore. Men and women prayed as the rocket line from the sea wall was fired time and time again towards the ships. Men and women grabbed hold of the rocket line to help pull it back in after it had missed its target, then fired out to the wreck again, if possible to save the drowning man. By 7p.m. the remainder of the crews from the wrecks were beyond anyone's help, the waves their temporary graves.

Shortly after high tide at 9 p.m. the brig *I.M.O.D.*, under Capt. Dobson, of Hartlepool, laden with coal, sailing to London, came into the harbour. She had lost her cookhouse, boats, galley, and part of their rigging. During the storm the deck had been constantly swept by the storm-raging sea constantly and her crew had been at the pumps without a rest and were exhausted.

During the night signals of distress were seen far out to sea. It is impossible to say how many vessels and lives were actually lost that day.

The following list is of those men known to have taken part as a crew-member in either the National lifeboat or the *Harbinger*, sometime during the day:

P. Anderson, S. Redhead, W. Miles, R. Scales, J. Brown, R. Cammish, E. Hutchinson, J. Stephenson, J. Ainsworth, J. Nicholls, J. Robinson, R. Hopper, R. Bedlington, Capt. G. Knott, J. Williamson, G. A. Knowsley, A. Miles, R. Williamson, J. Wallis, J. Usher, A. Bullock, T. Boddy, M. Walkington. And those that were lost R. Pickering, J. Clappison, R. Atkin, J. Watson, D. Purdon, W. Cobb.

As the next day dawned the beach presented a harrowing sight, littered with parts of ship hulls, spars, beams, sails, wood of all description in some places nine feet high, coal, anchors, chain, rope, personal belongings, a boot, a sou'wester, a ragged shirt half covered in sand, also a child's blue dress, ships papers belonging to the *Teresita*, of Harwich. Close to the pier were the bottom ribs of two or three vessels in different states of destruction. Most of the vessels had been colliers. Large quantities of coal were washed along the shoreline, and the sea ran black for weeks. During the previous night six bodies had been washed ashore. By noon, Saturday, 11 February, 11 bodies had been recovered from the shoreline. All were taken to the *Albion Inn*, which had been specially prepared for that purpose, being the largest building close to the South Beach. As you entered the yard at the back of the *Albion* the first sight for any visitor, were the tattered clothes, which had been removed from the bodies of their unfortunate seamen, hanging from the lines, saturated with salt water and covered with sand. Each body was carefully washed, before being placed in its coffin. Other bodies were washed ashore that weekend. By Sunday evening, 19 men and youths were laid side by side, many without any identification. One was identified as James Watson, one of the *Harbinger* lifeboat crew. He had gone off, three or four times in the boat, only missing one voyage, when he had gone home to put on some dry clothes, before returning to his position as a crew-member on the next launch. Other bodies had Shipwrecked Mariners Society tokens on them bearing numbers – 13,884 and 29,008 – by which they could be named. Each body was photographed with a view to identification at a later date, when news of the tragedy reached the homes of sailors whose ships were known to have been lost off the Yorkshire coast, and whose families visit Bridlington searching for their loved ones.

On Tuesday afternoon of 14 February, all the shops in the town had closed. At 2 o'clock the bodies, in their plain black coffins, were placed upon rulleys (flat four-wheeled horse-drawn wagon) and moved off from the *Albion Inn*, where the bodies had been carefully tended. The funeral procession was joined at the top of King Street by the funeral of James Watson, which had left from his home in Regent Terrace. The funeral cortège moved off in the following order: Chief Lord of the Manor, Chief Officer of Coastguards, Lloyds agent, representative of the National Lifeboat Institution, representative of the Shipwrecked Mariners Society, Medical Gentlemen, Ministers of All Denominations, Tradesmen of the Town, Committee and members of the Sailors and Working Men's Club, Missionary of the Port of Hull Society, Bridlington Amicable Society. James Watson's body was carried by lifeboat men, his coffin covered by a union flag, cabs with relatives, Members of the Ancient Order of Foresters, then six rulleys bearing 22 captains and seamen, the coffins being covered with union flags and other colours, followed by cabs carrying relatives and friends. As the cortège travelled along Prospect Street and St Johns Street towards the Priory many townsfolk joined the procession along the way, passing under the archway of the old Baylegate Gate. Approaching Bridlington Priory the mass of people stood respectfully aside for the

9. *The funeral courtege stopped at the top of King Street, February 1871, on the way to the Priory. The building on the right hand side is now a branch of Barclays Bank.*

main procession to pass through into the parish church of St Mary's for the church service, after which the quiet churchyard at Bridlington Priory received 23 bodies of the drowned sailors. James Watson was laid to rest in a grave near the north porch, three captains in one grave, and 19 seamen were laid to rest in part of the church yard, recently added at the expense of an old sailor, Capt. Beauvais RN, for the purpose of burying sailors, who might die or be washed ashore, drowned, at Bridlington.

It is known that 23 ships were driven ashore and wrecked in Bridlington Bay. Other ships were wrecked along the east coast of Yorkshire including, Spurn, Hornsea and Barmston. In total it is thought that in excess of 30 ships were lost.

No exact number is known of those who lost their lives from the shipwrecks that day. It is thought to be about seventy. Bodies continued to wash ashore for some weeks. They were interred in the churchyard. The burial register of Bridlington Priory for 1871 records each one as 'Drowned in Bridlington Bay', then the name of the wrecked ship or, if this was unknown, 'In the great storm of 10th Feb 1871'.

The following vessels were known to have been wrecked: the *John*, from Whitstable, the *Lavinia*, from Seaham, the *Teresita*, from Harwich, the *Spinner*, from Blyth, crew saved. The *Agility*, from North Shields, crew saved. The *Friends Increase*, from London, crew saved. The *Echo*, from Maldon, crew saved. The *Squirrel*, from Whitby, crew saved. The *Worthy*, from Lynn, crew saved. The *Peri*, from Lynn, crew saved. The *Margaret*, from Ipswich, Capt. and one crewman lost. The *Rebecca and Elizabeth*, from Lowestoft, crew saved. The *Bebside*, from Blyth, crew saved. The *Urina*, from Middlesbrough, crew saved. The *Vivid*, from Scarborough, crew saved. The *William Maitland*, from Whitby, all hands lost but the Capt. The *Caroline*, from Yarmouth, the Capt. and mate saved. The *Produce*, from Folkestone, four lost, two crewmen saved. The *Windsor*, from Lynn, crew saved. The *Arrow* from Sunderland, three crewmen lost. The *Delta*, from Whitby, all hands lost. Many other unknown vessels foundered with all hands.

A widow of one of the drowned men, whose body was found on the beach, sent the following letter, to the local paper, as an expression of her gratitude.

I am at a loss to express my gratitude to Mrs Knaggs and to the people of Bridlington Quay, for their kindness and assistance under my present trying circumstances. My dear departed husband was one of the crew of the brig *Delta*, of Whitby, which was lost with all her crew in Bridlington Bay on the 10th February last. Mrs Knagg's Telegraphed to Hartlepool, to say that a body had been found, and that the Fishermen and Shipwrecked Mariners Society medal, on the body, was marked T. Jameson, of Hartlepool. Mrs Knagg's brother immediately informed me, and very kindly reply for me, after I described my inability to perform the journey, also my circumstances, I requested Mrs Knagg's to see that the body of my dear husband was interred, which she very kindly attended to. To my great and grateful surprise, I received by postal order from Mrs Knagg's, contributed by her self and other friends the sum of £1, 11 shillings and sixpence. Later by rail, carriage paid, the following articles, which were found on the body of my dear husband, the Shipwrecked Mariners Society medal on which was his name, a knife, tobacco pouch, and a sixpence, along with a letter with particulars of the funeral. On the following day I received another kind letter enclosing a few more shillings. A space in your valuable paper will give me the desired privilege of returning my sincere thanks to all friends at Bridlington Quay for the above named kindness.

Your humble servant,

L. Jameson, 12 Olive Street, Hartlepool, April 25th 1871.

Forty-three bodies of those who lost their lives that day are buried in the churchyard at the Priory Church, Bridlington.

A monument, paid for by public subscriptions, was erected over the mass grave in the Priory churchyard in memory of the lifeboat men and seamen who lost their lives. The four sides are engraved with these words:

ON THE NORTH FACE
The Arrow of Sunderland
The Caroline of Yarmouth
The Delta of Whitby
The John of Whitstable
The Lavinia of Seaham
The Margaret of Ipswich
The Produce of Folkestone
The Teresita of Harwich
The William Maitland of Whitby
AND AN UNKNOWN ENGLISH
SCHOONER WERE WRECKED ON THE
10TH FEBRUARY 1871, WITH LOSS OF
LIFE IN BRIDLINGTON BAY
THIRTEEN OTHER VESSELS WERE
LOST IN THE BAY IN THE SAME GALE

ON THE EAST FACE
In Lasting Memory
of
A Great company of Seamen
who perished in the fearful Gale
which swept over
Bridlington Bay
on February 10th 1871
The waves of the sea are
Mighty and rage horribly but
The Lord who dwelleth on high
is Mightier

ON THE SOUTH FACE
In Remembrance of
Robert Pickering
John Clappison
Richard Atkin
James Watson
David Purdon
William Cobb

ON THE WEST FACE
Forty-Three Bodies
Of those who on that day
lost their lives lie in this
Church Yard

Who lost their lives in the
Harbinger Lifeboat
Whilst nobly endeavouring to
Save those whose bodies rest
Below

The following poem was published in a local newspaper two days after the tragic event

The Storm in Bridlington Bay, 1871
The ocean roars with mighty voice aloud,
The sky is darkened with the storm-rode cloud,
Out in the Bay the labouring barque is seen,
By breaker after breaker is her deck swept clean,
Her crew, be numbed with cold, have climbed the mast,
Her tiller jammed, towards shore she's drifting fast,
Each moment seemed as if it would be her last,
It must not be, for down upon the sand,
Is gathering fast a stalwart hardy band,
They man the lifeboat; quick it stems the tide,
With hearty will the bending oar is plied,
On towering wave they near the fated ship,
And then beneath the watery wall they dip,
As on the foaming surge again they rise,
They can see their comrades; they can hear their cries,
Alas! In vain! The same engulfing wave,
Opens for them a ready yawning grave.

***

No more your wives shall wait for your return,
No more your children's love for you shall burn,
True Britons, ye have not your name belied,
For saving others, ye yourselves have died.
A.E.B. Feb.12th 1871.

The entry from the Harbour Master's Log, 10 February 1871:

A light breeze from the Eastward and cloudy, at 2 am. E.S.E., fresh. At 8 am. Blowing a heavy gale with snow and sleet and a heavy sea, many ships came onshore, lifeboat saved many hands but many were drowned, lifeboat upset and six were drowned out of her, latter part more moderate.

As a direct result of the disaster, and supported by appeals from the residents of Flamborough, in November 1871 the RNLI established the Flamborough lifeboat stations, one at North Landing and the second at South Landing.

Each year for 100 years, an annual service of remembrance, attended by the Mayor at Bridlington, the crews of Bridlington and Flamborough lifeboats and representatives of many other organisations, was held at the Priory Church on the nearest Sunday to 10 February. Following the service a short pilgrimage was made to the memorial in the churchyard. The last specially organised service to feature civic representatives was held in 1971, the centenary of the disaster.

In 1976, my first February as coxswain, I managed, with the help of the Rev. Nolan of the Priory Church, to revive interest in what I believe is one of the most important events in the history of our town, which should never be forgotten. The late Rev. J Meek continued to help, and today the Rev. J. Wardle carries on this work. The memorial service is combined with the normal morning service at the Priory Church on the nearest Sunday to the 10th of February each year, when the Bridlington lifeboat crews, families and helpers attend and remember the devastation that struck Bridlington Bay, the way the whole town pulled together to help save lives, and the sacrifice given by the lifeboat men of Bridlington Quay, on 10 February 1871.

The Aftermath of the Great Gale

On the following Tuesday a meeting was called by Mr George Richardson, the Chief Lord, in the Victoria Rooms. The purpose of the meeting was to help with relief to those suffering and reward the heroic work of the Bridlington Quay lifeboat men during the 10 February great storm. The Chief Lord chaired the meeting. The Rev. James Thomson, Rev. J. Dickinson, E.R. Harding, D.R.W. Porritt, RNLI, The Secretary for Bridlington Quay, T. Harland, R.D. Preston, J.W. Postill and Capt. Morris were also on the platform. Calling the meeting to order, the chairman said he was at a loss to describe the awful calamity and terrible loss of life, which had occurred on Friday 10 February. No living person had ever witnessed such an event. Money could not replace those sacrificed, but he was pleased to announce that the amount to be collected would go a long way to help the widows and families. Acknowledging the heroic efforts that had been made by the lifeboat men of the Quay, a cheque for £5 had this morning arrived from Worksop. The Rev. Y. Lloyd Greame said he believed the crew did all they could; large amounts are being raised through subscriptions at Leeds and Sheffield and £200 is likely to be raised at Hull; other towns are doing likewise. A committee shall be formed to help with the relief of the widows and orphans of those who were lost.

Mr R.D. Preston remarked, 'They may as well not give money, unless some way was found to prevent such a tragic loss of life, if the storm of such ferocity should visit the Bay again.' Answering, Mr. Porritt said he didn't see what more could have been done, both lifeboats had done the best, Coxswain James Stephenson had been in the boat all day, most of the crews had worn the skin off their hands, through the task of rowing the lifeboats out into the Bay time and time again, in an effort to save the crews from the wrecks. Mr Porritt added he had asked Captain Ward, the inspector for the RNLI, to hold an inquiry. The chairman then announced that the Rev. Y. Lloyd Greame had agreed to fund a new lifeboat for Bridlington Quay. The meeting then closed.

As a result of Mr Porritt's request, a meeting was convened on 15 February at the Sailors and Working Men's Club. Captain Ward attended to meet with the sailors and fishermen and to hear their thoughts and experiences of the RNLI old lifeboat, or the present one which was self-righting, the modern design. It was the RNLI custom, said Captain Ward, to send an inspector to make inquiries, if any station was dissatisfied with their boat, or loss of life had taken place. The Institute had a fleet of lifeboats consisting of two kinds, the old design considered very safe, wide beam with curved keels, and then the self-righting ones, the same as the one stationed here at the Quay. Mr James Stephenson, coxswain of the *Robert Whitworth* lifeboat was asked how she had performed on the 10th. She had acted well and, he said, until the last trip. Against a strong wind and a flood tide with a heavy sea she couldn't be launched. The crew gave their opinions. One said the boat was too high out of the water and lively, and the action of the boat was liable to cause oars to be broken whilst rowing. The old boat was better to handle in and out of the water. Another crew member, William Miles, second coxswain, preferred the present boat, it being very safe. George Chaplin preferred the old boat. G. Dixon together with J. Lyon objected to the rudder as it required the boat to turn around in order to pull back ashore, which the old boat didn't, being double ended and could be steered from either end, as the Greathead design. Each seaman giving his opinion, most of the men had crewed in the lifeboats for years. Captain Ward answered the main criticism about the RNLI boat. The RNLI make paramount importance the safety of all its lifeboat crews, and cutting down and making the boat lighter might result in a weaker boat construction, thereby increasing the danger to the crews in bad weather.

The RNLI had in the past seen 30 of their lifeboats capsize; all but one had self righted without any loss of life, which is why the RNLI had been committed to self-righting lifeboats. The chairman then asked John Robinson, coxswain of the *Harbinger*, how she had handled. He stated the boat acted as a surf boat to perfection, easy to row, enabling them to save the crews of six vessels, safe until the heavy sea and tide caught her causing the capsize. The chairman asked Robinson, if the crew had been wearing lifebelts would they all have survived; 'yes' he said. Captain Ward added, 'All lifeboat crews should wear a lifebelt, like the ones supplied to RNLI lifeboat crews, invented by myself.' Mr Wallace remarked that when lifebelts are worn in the boat, they also protect the chest from the cold as well as strong blows, when the lifeboat is buffeted by a storm-tossed sea. The meeting then went on to discuss the build of each of the lifeboats, clinker built or carvel, self-righting or none self-righting.

At the end of the meeting the chairman put forward the following proposals.

Would you prefer:
(1) a lifeboat built on the old system with improvements and modifications
(2) the present style of lifeboat with modifications and improvements
(3) a boat of any other build?

A vote was then taken: for the first proposal there were 38 votes; for the second there were 7 votes; for the third, no votes.

The ledger of the RNLI records:

February the 10th – A fearful gale took place on this part of the coast on which occasion the RNLI. lifeboat succeeded in saving crews consisting of 16 men from three wrecked vessels.

A private lifeboat, which had been presented to the boat men by Count Gustave Batthyany had put off several times and saved a number of lives from different vessels, but on the seventh time she unhappily capsized and drowned six of the crew.

February the 11th – Inspector visited station in order to make inquiries into the whole circumstances of the case. Attended in the evening a meeting of the local inhabitants, which had been convened to organise a form for the relief of the widows and orphans of the drowned men. The Rev. Y. Lloyd Greame, a gentleman of fortune, residing in the neighbourhood, stated that as the boatman had informed him, that the small lifeboat, which had been capsized, was only suited for services to vessels in shallow water, near the shore, and that the Institute's lifeboat could not have been propelled against a heavy sea and gale of wind. He had promised to give the men a new lifeboat fully equipped which they should select for themselves. A great many of the boatmen were present at this meeting.

February the 13th – In the morning the inspector attended a meeting of the local committee at which Mr Lloyd Greame and the 1st and 2nd coxswains of the Institute's lifeboat were present. The coxswain stated that the boat had saved 16 lives from the vessels but that all attempts to reach the fourth wreck failed although they persevered for about two hours, becoming exhausted. They however had great confidence in the boat and would not exchange her either for the small boat or for the one the Institute took away some years ago.

   Mr Greame repeated his promise to give a new lifeboat and said he would prefer that the institution should undertake the management of it but that he could not depart from his agreement that it was to be a boat, which the boatmen should approve of. Subsequently all the boatmen in the place, with the exception of seven, two being the coxswains of the institution's lifeboat, decided in favour of a non self-righting lifeboat, all the inspector's arguments in favour of self-righting plan, having failed to convince them of its advantages over the other class of lifeboats.

   The inspector therefore recommended, that the institution should undertake the management of the new boat, which Mr Lloyd Greame was about to present to the men. The responsibility of selecting among self righting lifeboats resting on the men themselves and not on the institution, and that the new boat and the present one be placed at a sufficient distance from one another to prevent one interfering with the efficiency of the other.

March the 2nd the RNLI committee in London declined to accept the responsibility of undertaking the management of such lifeboat as that proposed to be presented by Mr Lloyd Greame. Committee voted 100 Guineas in aid of the fund, for the relief of widows and orphans, of the drowned men, and to reward the crews of the private lifeboat, saving a number of lives on the understanding that not more than 20 Guineas of the amount to be devoted to the latter object.

March the 3rd forward the draft for £105 to Honorary Secretary accordingly with a communication explained the decision and wishes of the committee.

March the 11th honorary secretary called at the institutions where Mr Lewis further explained to him, the decision of the committee, with which he entirely agreed.

May the 15th – Emmet and Emmet, solicitors of Halifax, forwarded to the institution a cheque for £2078 13 shillings and 11p, being the amount of the legacy and interest thereon bequeathed to the RNLI by the late *John Abbott* Esq., for the purpose of placing a lifeboat on the Yorkshire coast to be named after the Testator.

June the 1st committee decided to place a new 31-foot lifeboat at Bridlington in lieu of the present boat and appropriated to the late Mr Abbott's legacy.

The recommendation from Captain Ward to the fishermen, that the RNLI should take over the management of the boat, given by Mr Lloyd Greame, had been overruled. As a result of the meeting the *Robert Whitworth*, which the men had agreed was not suited to the conditions in Bridlington Bay, was replaced. She was re-stationed at Carnsore, County Wexford, Ireland, and given a new name *Iris*, where she was launched on 20 occasions to wrecks saving 73 lives, until being withdrawn from service in 1890. She proved to be a good boat for the deep water and rugged coastline of that area.

The Lifeboat *John Abbott*

She was replaced by the *John Abbott*. The legacy had been used as requested to provide a lifeboat to be stationed on the Yorkshire coast. The greatest skill and care had gone into her building, to ensure she should be in every way suited to the requirements of the men who were to crew her. She was 34 feet long, 7 feet 6 inches beam, had ten oars, to be double-banked if required (two men to pull on each oar to provide extra power for the boat if it was needed, in this event the crew would be made up of 23 men.) She was sharper in the bow, which would enable her to be rowed far more easily against heavy seas than the *Robert Whitworth*. Her stability trials had taken place in Regent's Canal dock, London. The water shipped, as the boat had been capsized by means of a crane, was self-ejected in 25 seconds after self-righting. Built by Messrs. Forrestt of Limehouse, London, at a cost of £263, she was fully equipped with a new transporting and launching carriage.

At 2 p.m. on 24 August 1871, the *John Abbott*, with a full crew on board, was pulled from the boathouse, at the junction of South Marine Drive and Railway Crescent (Windsor Crescent) by six horses, through the town to the North Beach to be launched. They were accompanied by Mr Rigg of Halifax, executor of the will of the late Mr Abbott, Captain Ward of the RNLI, Mr Porritt RNLI secretary, Major Wilkinson with members of the volunteer life company, together with a large number of visitors and townspeople. On the North Beach the procession halted for a short formal ceremony. Mr Rigg officially presented the boat to the RNLI which he believed was built from the best materials possible and was ready for its work and he hoped it would never be wanted to save human life. Captain Ward accepted the boat saying he had the honour to represent the RNLI, who had 230 lifeboats, 34 of which were stationed along the north-east coast of England, most of which had been donated by people living away from the coast. Miss Barnes (daughter of Captain Barnes of Sewerby Crescent) broke a bottle of wine on her bow, naming the lifeboat *John Abbott* and wishing her Godspeed in her work of mercy. The boat was then launched, the crew putting her through her paces, under oar and sail. (This is the first mention of any means of propulsion other than rowing in a Bridlington lifeboat.) The boat performed well. Miss Barnes and several gentlemen were carried in the boat on its first launch. Appreciation was shown to Captain Ward for his efforts to change the old boat as the boatman had requested.

The damage to the *Harbinger* sustained on 10 February was repaired. Her management was agreed to be undertaken by the Sailors and Working Men's Club, which had been formed in February 1865.

Count G. Batthyany sent a letter to the club, of which he was a Vice President, stating that when the *Harbinger* was placed in the hands of the club he would present a launching and transporting carriage suitable for the *Harbinger* so that her efficiency would be increased.

R.D. Preston Esq. said he would present a set of lifebelts for the crew, provided they were kept at his house.

Both offers were gladly accepted by the club.

The *Harbinger* was to be used by the fishermen as before the great gale, not only as a lifeboat but also as a general workboat. The committee stated that the *Harbinger* should receive 5 per cent of any salvage claim, the value of which was above £3.03 per man; for all sums under that amount, as is the custom with the cobles, one share of all earnings. The boat was and should be at the service of any sailor of fishermen on these terms. Fishermen earned their living from the sea so salvage was lucrative. There was great competition to get to a boat in distress. If the master of a ship took a line, you then had the right to a share of the value of the ship and cargo. Fishermen would get a line on board the vessel in distress and then either get on board and sail the ship into harbour, or, if the boat was grounded, they could help get it off, to earn a reward from the ship's owners.

The *Harbinger* was to be moored in the harbour and in such a place as the committee thought best. In every case where the boat sustained any damage when on service, the damage was to be reported to the sub-committee or any member thereof so that she may be repaired as soon as possible. The boat on returning from service was not to be left in the surf or on the beach, but must be got on to her carriage or to her mooring as soon as possible. This leads us to believe that sometimes she was moored in the harbour, other times ashore on her carriage. It is known that later in her life she was housed in 'Raff Yard' (an area where planks of fir and pine timber were stored), later Princess Street and now the Promenade's shopping centre.

Volunteer Life Company

As a direct result of a lack of trained manpower to help with the rocket and mortar apparatus during the great gale, the Volunteer Life Company was formed to co-operate with coastguards, in trying to establish rapid communications from the land with vessels in distress. For some years, the rocket and mortar apparatus to project lines across stranded ships had been under the care of the coastguards stationed at Bridlington, and to work it properly 15 men were required. On 10 February, Mr Tyrrel, the chief coastguard, attended to the duties from 9 a.m. to 8 p.m. with only five men, all of the coastguards stationed at Bridlington at that time. The company of volunteers was consequently formed on 21 March 1871, whose object, as its name implies, was to save life. Thirty members enrolled, not counting the coastguards stationed at Bridlington. Each member found his own uniform and they had regular practices four times a year, with rocket and mortar apparatus. The company was under the regulations of the coastguards. The formation of the company resulted from the exertions of Major C.B. Wilkinson, an officer living in Bridlington, who served with great honour in the 68th Light Infantry in the Crimean campaign, for which he received two medals and four clasps.

In December 1885 plans were drawn up for a building in West Street to be used by the Volunteer Life Company (today the Toc H). It was called the Rocket Cart House. In this building was kept all their lifesaving equipment, rocket guns and apparatus together with the cart used for its transportation to the site of any wreck.

Part of the Volunteer Life Company was subsequently formed into a volunteer fire brigade for the town. In 1894 it became full-time. The rest went on to become the Rocket Brigade later to form what is today the Auxiliary Coastguard unit.

3

The *Seagull* Lifeboat and its Rivals

The offer by the Rev. Yarburgh Lloyd Greame of Sewerby House to provide a lifeboat for the Quay gave the fishermen and boatmen an opportunity to look at a variety of lifeboat models obtained from around the coast. Models of these boats had been on exhibition in the Victoria Sailors and Working Men's clubhouse for 14 days, at the end of which each seaman in turn passed the model boats, depositing a token in the design he thought the best one suited to the conditions at Bridlington. The result of this ballot was, John Ainsworth boat 2, Appledore boat 6, Filey boat 8, Tyne boat 23 votes. The Tyne boat was preferred by a majority of nearly two-thirds.

This lifeboat design harked back to the design of the first Bridlington lifeboat of the Greathead design and its replacement, built at Scarborough by Skelton. Both had been well-liked boats for their performance at sea. The new boat was built on the lines of the Shields pilot boat, with very minor changes, by Dodgin and Co. of North Shields at a cost of £245.

The *Seagull* Lifeboat

Her dimensions were: length 28 feet, beam 9 feet 9 inches, depth 3 feet 8 inches. The full cost together with its carriage, boathouse and land on which the boathouse was to be built was £800. The draft of the boat in the sea, with a double crew of 24 men plus the coxswain, was 17 inches. Mr W. Smithson built the transporting and launching carriage in Bridlington. Its length was 22 feet, width 5½ feet, width of wheels six inches (to help prevent, due to the weight, boat and carriage sinking into the sand) and it was made with eight metal rollers in the keel way and made to tip when launching. The carriage was fitted with a block and tackle system to pull the boat off the carriage when launching into the sea. The total weight with a crew of 12 was five tonnes.

The boat, after being reluctantly turned down by the RNLI committee, as it was not built according to the RNLI's stringent specifications and did not feature self-righting properties, was offered to the Sailors and Working Men's Club in Cliff Street, who willingly took on the management and responsibility for her. They purchased the two wooden shops and land on the Promenade side next to the club, to build the new boathouse. The boat arrived in Bridlington in early October 1871 but not until 26 December 1871 was she named. This was because the crew, having exercised the boat in the Bay, found some snags in her build. The air boxes in the centre of the boat

10. *The* Seagull *lifeboat, possibly at its naming ceremony, 26 December 1871. Note the bunches of holly adorning the boat, especially the stern.*

were in the way of the men rowing. The coxswain W. Clark said the steering rollock was too high, the steering oar four feet too long and the grating for the steersman four inches too high. A loose thwart fore and aft for two more men would be an improvement. The sub-committee resolved to have the air cases removed to the sides at once and the alterations would be carried out by local well-known boat builder Mr Siddall. He found that the air cases were not built to plan: both leaked and the lifeline eyebolts were imperfect and unsafe. The screw valve in the ballast tank was defective. The builders Messrs Dodgin and Co. were written to. They replied saying that they would send the steamer *United Services* to tow the *Seagull* back to the Tyne where they could overhaul her and the snags would be put right.

On her return to the town, her naming ceremony took place. On Tuesday, 26 December 1871 at 10 a.m., six horses, pulling the lifeboat on its carriage, headed the procession, to take the boat from the boathouse in Cliff Street through the town before travelling up St John Street to High Street and to Major Prickett's house 'The Avenue'. (Later this building became a Bridlington hospital, part of which was the maternity hospital where many local people including myself and my two sons were born.)

The procession then moved on to High Green Dyke (a Large Pond on High Green) into which the lifeboat was launched. With a full crew of 12 oarsmen and two coxswains, all wearing cork lifejackets, an imaginary rescue was acted out, saving the crew from a shipwreck, for the pleasure of the crowds.

Within sight of these events was the quiet, peaceful churchyard of the Priory, the last resting-place of those who had been so tragically lost, only months before, on 10 February.

The boat was re-carriaged before proceeding to Sewerby House (now called Sewerby Hall), the home of the Rev. Yarburgh Lloyd Greame, benefactor of the boat, arriving there at 12 noon. After a short introduction the vicar of Sewerby, the Rev. M. Tylee, offered prayers and the blessing of the Almighty upon the boat, that it might be a means of saving life by Him who commanded the wind and the seas be still. The Rev. Y. Lloyd Greame then introduced his daughter, Miss Greame, who proceeded to name the lifeboat *Seagull*, dashing a glass of wine over the bow of the boat amidst the cheers of the crowd. The Rev. Lloyd Greame explained that it was on seeing the awful spectacle of so many brave fellows perishing during the fearful gale, that had led him into paying for the *Seagull* lifeboat and he hoped that the men called upon to man her would have every confidence in her qualities.

> Now it gives me great pleasure to give the *Seagull* Life, handing her into the safe keeping of the hands of the Trustees of the Sailors and Working Men's Club. I hope it will be a long time before she is wanted, but should such a time come I hope that like a seagull she would be riding safe on the ocean waves and be the means of saving many lives.

Secretary Mr J.W. Postill, who thanked the reverend benefactor for 'the most precious and magnificent gift', gratefully received the *Seagull* on behalf of the Working Men's Club. Mr J. Robinson, one of the survivors of the *Harbinger* disaster, said he believed the boat was an excellent one. She only wanted to be well manned to go through any danger: 'May God protect the family of Lloyd Greame forever, for this great and magnificent gift'.

Mr Harding, Vice-President of the Working Men's Club, Captain Lloyd Greame, son of the benefactor, and Mr J. Wallace, coxswain of the lifeboat, all delivered speeches before the lifeboat was transported back to the boathouse via Marton Hall, where she was taken to allow the Misses Creyke to look her over.

By the end of 1871, Bridlington had three lifeboats available to save lives at sea: the *Seagull*, the *Harbinger* and the *John Abbott*.

On 17 February 1872, at a meeting of seamen, it was proposed that Mr M. W. Clark be elected as coxswain for the *Seagull* lifeboat. The vote was carried unanimously, only fishermen and seamen being allowed a vote.

The RNLI boat the *John Abbott*, known locally as the National Lifeboat, had its upkeep funded from Headquarters in London. This caused considerable bitterness and rivalry between the local fishermen and the Institution. It was thought to be a scandal that the Working Men's Club should have to maintain the lifeboat while the RNLI contributed nothing to the upkeep and running of the *Seagull*. Visitors to the town showed great admiration for her and gave generously towards her upkeep. The *Seagull* lifeboat became very popular, often showing superiority, when at sea, over the National Lifeboat.

This was apparent on 5 March 1874, during a gale from the south-east with frequent heavy showers of rain and a heavy sea running. A vessel approaching the shore near Wilsthorpe was showing signals of distress. She drifted towards the town, passing the North Pier about half a mile out. The *Seagull* and the RNLI boat were taken to Sand Cut, at the bottom of Sands Lane, where both boats were launched and, with difficulties, made their way through the heavy shore break to the vessel, heavy seas continually forcing them back. The vessel was the brigantine *Nelson* with a crew of five men; she was carrying a cargo of copper ore, which had moved during the gale, rendering the vessel uncontrollable. The crew were rescued by the *Seagull* and brought safely to shore. Although honour fell to the *Seagull*, it was thought that no spirit of rivalry was occasioned among the brave sailors in both lifeboats, who both had a common interest in saving human life.

Again, on 7 and 8 December 1874, three of the fishing cobles belonging to the Quay had a very narrow escape whilst fishing at sea. A strong breeze came up and so produced a heavy sea. Seas breaking over her twice filled the *Lavinia* belonging to R. Crawford and the crew had great difficulty in keeping her afloat. The crew of the coble *Isaiah* took refuge on a yawl towing the coble safely into harbour, while the crew of the other coble were taken on board the *Little Jenny* and the coble was cast adrift. The *Harbinger* went out twice to render assistance in case of an accident. In recognition of the service T.W. Palmer of Brough, who was staying at the Quay, gave the Coxswain, Mr W. Clark, two guineas to be handed out among the crew. The fact that the boat was kept moored at the entrance to the harbour exposed to all weathers and ready for immediate service and that the expense attending to it and the *Seagull*, has to be borne by an institution maintained entirely by working men may become better known, enlisting the aid of occasional visitors and inducing well-to-do townspeople to contribute regularly to the fund for the maintenance of these two boats to be kept thoroughly equipped for any emergency.

On 8 November 1878, during the early morning, six fishing cobles left Bridlington harbour for the purpose of long line fishing for cod, to the south. The moderate wind was blowing from the south-west. During the middle of the day the wind veered to the north, increasing to a violent gale. Three of the cobles left the fishing grounds early, managing with considerable difficulty to reach the safety of the harbour, as they had to beat (sail) up against the violence of the storm. The other three boats were unable to make the harbour as the northerly storm increased. The cobles were *Annie* crewed by George Wallace and Edward Miles, the *Nellie* crewed by William Naggs, Melsh Walkington and J. Lawson; the third coble was called the *Stranger*, crewed by William Welburn, Andrew Wilson and Richard Purvis. Due to the ebbing tide and violence of the storm these cobles could not make headway towards the harbour so decided to run their boats onto the beach near Barmston. After encountering great difficulties the *Nellie* and *Annie* managed to run onto the beach and safety; the *Stranger* was less fortunate. Whilst going through a heavy breaking surf some distance from the shore, she was capsized by a heavy sea which threw her crew into the boiling surf. Wilson and Purvis managed to save themselves by clinging to the broken mast and oars and succeeded in reaching the shore. William Welburn after struggling for some time was overcome by the mighty waves; he sank and was drowned. His body was washed ashore at Mappleton.

He was later described as a man of excellent character, a hard worker and careful man who owned his own coble. William's body was interred in the grounds of the

Priory Church, only seven years after the Great Gale of 1871. He left a pregnant widow and four children, the youngest of whom was Ernest, aged 18 months. Ernest later became lifeboat coxswain at Bridlington and as did his son, George William 'Brannie' Welburn.

Purvis, Wallis, Welburn, Walkington, these men or relatives of these men were coxswains of the Bridlington lifeboat for over 94 years.

Barmston Lifeboat Station

About 6 p.m. on 6 March 1883 a flare was seen from a vessel riding at anchor, about a mile east-south-east from the harbour on shoal ground. A strong gale from the north was blowing, together with thick snow showers and a heavy sea. A flare was shown at intervals until midnight when the vessel parted and slipped her anchor. Shortly afterwards a vessel, supposed to be the same one, showed a flare again, south of the piers. The coxswain answered from shore sending up two rockets. Then the crew mustered and horses were got together. The vessel, however, hove away to the south and nothing more was seen of her. The coxswain did not fetch out the boat to the vessel when she was riding at anchor because there was too much wind and sea to board the vessel. As the sea was breaking round her the hatch had been secured. The lifeboat could not have been launched nearer than eight or nine miles to the south of Bridlington; the gale was one of remarkable severity. The tide would have been in flood when the lifeboat reached the South Beach. Had he succeeded in getting her off and so high up the beach, that coxswain said it would have been difficult if not impossible to get back at shore.

The coxswain had mustered the crew, but due to the severe weather conditions had been unable to launch and rescue the crew of the *Matchless*.

As a result of this shipwreck and others that had occurred in the same area, some miles to the south of Bridlington, the RNLI decided to open a lifeboat station at Barmston. Several vessels had gone ashore in this locality at different times. One year before the *Matchless*, a vessel was wrecked in the immediate vicinity and went down with all hands. It was then urged by the residents of Bridlington Quay, the nearest lifeboat station, that it would be most desirable to establish an auxiliary station at Barmston, the boat to be manned by a crew from Bridlington, in the absence of competent seamen in the village of Barmston or the surrounding area.

The lifeboat to be stationed there had been bequeathed by the late George Walker Esq. of Southport: £3,100 for the establishment and permanent endowment of a lifeboat for the Yorkshire coast, to be named the *George and Jane Walker*, having been appropriated for that purpose. The lifeboat provided was one of the 34 feet, 10-oar class, built by Forrestt at Limehouse, London and was furnished with the transporting carriage. She was to be manned by coxswain, second coxswain, bowman and 10 oarsmen. Sir Henry Boynton gave the land on which to build a boathouse. The full cost of establishing the station was almost £1,000. On the completion of the boathouse, in September 1884, the public inauguration of the station took place in the presence of a large concourse of spectators, under the direction of Mr A. West, Honorary Secretary of Bridlington lifeboat. The boat was successfully launched under the charge of Cdr Carter RN, district inspector of lifeboats. The *George and Jane Walker* was the first

11. The Barmston lifeboat, 1884

Bridlington lifeboat to have an official RNLI number: O.N.10. Prior to 1833 this had not been considered necessary. From 1833 all lifeboats had to recover from being capsized with all gear onboard except sails, so each new lifeboat was given an official number, which continues to this day.

To station a lifeboat at Barmston was a bold decision by the RNLI, knowing that, without any fishermen or seamen living in the village, the crew would have to be from Bridlington. But would be saved by only having to transport the crew men from Bridlington rather than the boat on its carriage, pulled by horses miles along the beach or even through the fields on the cliff top. This was a unique step forward for the men of Bridlington, being responsible for a lifeboat in another village along the coast.

Bridlington men now formed the crews of four lifeboats. The *John Abbott, Seagull,* the *Harbinger,* and the *George and Jane Walker* at Barmston.

The rivalry between the teams of lifeboat crew-members continued, even when the men mixed and matched to make up the crew or helpers for each of the other boats. The talk of who had the best lifeboat for the job continued and the rivalry between the national lifeboat, which had proved not to be the boat for this area, and the private lifeboats of Bridlington continued. But each boat was used to its best advantage. This rivalry was the same as between any teams today, one trying to prove that they were better than the other, but the over-riding fact was that nothing ever got in the way of saving the lives of others.

This rivalry was highlighted by Alfred West, Secretary for the national boat, in his report for a lifeboat service launch. On 6 December 1881 at about 8.00p.m. distress flares were seen at intervals to the south and apparently getting nearer. When it was known that the vessel would be wrecked, the lifeboat, which had been ready with horses for about an hour, was taken to the North Beach. The wind was south-south-west Force 8 with a heavy sea and a strong ebb tide. On the beach the coxswain, George Dixon, considered it was not possible to reach the vessel against the tide and wind. At 10 o'clock, the tide having eased, the national boat was launched and the *Seagull* lifeboat tried to launch but failed. There was strong rivalry between the two lifeboats. Mr West reported that the cost of horses was expensive; 15 shillings per horse was paid, which would have been the same rate of pay as the rocket apparatus. The Institution's *John Abbott* was launched an hour before the *Seagull*. The latter failed to launch for the most part because the horses were unaccustomed to, or unsuitable for, the work. The *New Eagle* was a Grimsby-registered boat, a sloop of 38 tons, carrying coal from Hartlepool to Burnham. Her sails had been blown away, and she was therefore at the mercy of the sea. Her crew of two were rescued by the lifeboat *John Abbott*. The lifeboat crew received 20 shillings each (£1 in today's currency).

In March 1885, while on a routine inspection of the Bridlington Station and its lifeboat, Cdr Carter of the RNLI had a meeting with the coxswain and crew, who explained to the inspector that they considered the present boat was built on too fine lines; they believed it was not the correct boat for the conditions in Bridlington Bay and was it possible to obtain a new National Lifeboat for Bridlington? Two weeks later Mr A. West, the Honorary Secretary, received a letter from the RNLI, agreeing to the wishes of the men.

Monday, 13 April 1885 saw a new lifeboat arrived at Bridlington, signalling the end of the *John Abbott*. She was taken away from Bridlington and later in that year she was condemned and broken up. She had been too light, built on too fine a line, and too small. Because of the rivalry she experienced with the *Seagull*, the *John Abbott* never became popular with the men. This reflected in her record – after 14 years' service at Bridlington, she had only launched on service six times, and saved two lives from the sloop *New Eagle* of Grimsby on 6 December 1881.

The *William John and Frances* 1885

The new lifeboat was called *William John and Frances* and cost £300 to build. This had been paid from a legacy of the late Mr. W. J. Payne of Reigate. She was self-righting, built by Woulfe of Shadwell in 1884. Built into her were all the latest improvements, including water ballast tanks. These qualities were subsequently to enable her, like her sister lifeboat at Barmston, to pass the revised RNLI self-righting test and to be allocated an official number, O.N.9. Her dimensions were similar to the *John Abbott's*, 34 feet by 7 feet 6 ins. She was built on much fuller lines and therefore looked considerably larger than her predecessor. Weighing 3.35 tons, she was heavier than the earlier Bridlington lifeboats.

On 8 December 1886, a heavy gale was blowing from the south-east, causing a heavy breaking swell on the beach. At 8 o'clock a vessel was reported driving onto the North Beach. She was the brig *Orb* from Whitby, on passage to Yarmouth carrying a cargo of coal. Shortly afterwards, she ran aground on the North Beach and was in immediate danger of breaking up. All three lifeboats were taken to the North Beach; the first one to arrive was the little *Harbinger*; the crew, being so eager to launch, took the lifebelts belonging to the crew of the *Seagull*. Was it taking longer for the *Seagull* and national boat to get to the launch site? On launching, the *Harbinger's* crew had great difficulty in rowing the lifeboat clear of the shore break, so great was the violence of the wind. She was nearly 20 years old, oars started to break one by one in the heavy seas, until they couldn't keep the boat moving forward. She had no sails and became helpless, being driven back onto the beach. The crew were saved by the *Seagull's* lifebelts. Waiting for them on the beach were the crew of the *Seagull*, claiming back the lifebelts before launching the *Seagull* lifeboat. At the same time the *William John and Frances* lifeboat was taken onto the North Beach and launched at the first attempt. Rowing into wind and sea, the crew could not reach the vessel. The crew, tired, became exhausted with their attempt and had to return to the beach. A fresh crew were, therefore, put into the boat. On the second attempt they managed to reach the vessel, saving the crew of nine men. The vessel became a total wreck.

Twenty-four men formed the two crews of the *William John and Frances* on the two launches. During the second launch, one man, John Dawson, was washed out of the lifeboat, but wearing a lifebelt succeeded in safely reaching the beach. Each lifeboat crew-member received 10 shillings. The five men who went on both launches were paid £1; the beach man, for assisting to launch and haul up the lifeboat, was paid four shillings. The owners of each of the eight horses used to the transport the lifeboat to the site of the wreck were paid 10 shillings. The lifeboat sustained slight damage, which was repaired locally. They also broke six oars when rowing through the heavy surf.

It would seem that the coxswain liked this boat and the crew. On being asked, how did the boat behave, during the service, the answer was 'well'.

When the *Orb*, was wrecked the ship's wheel was purchased by a visitor to the town, Mrs E. L. Chawner, who then presented it to Mr P. Anderson of the Sailors Bethel. Today, the ship's wheel is still in Bridlington. The Sailors Bethel has moved several times since that day and changed its name to The Harbourside Evangelical Church. The wheel, thankfully, still holds pride of place in the church.

The committee of the Bridlington Sailors and Working Men's Institute held a committee meeting to consider the state of the *Harbinger* lifeboat. It was reported by the Secretary that the lifeboat committee and the seamen of the town met to consider the state of the *Harbinger*, as to her safety and future use. A number of men had examined the boat and they unanimously agreed with the opinion expressed by the coxswain, George Wallis, that the boat had run her course and was not of any further use as a lifeboat. It was decided to request the committee to dispose of the boat and her outfits and pay the proceeds into the lifeboat fund, the *Seagull* fund.

The *Harbinger* was taken to Stamford Bridge to do service as a house boat. Later it was taken to Kirkham Abbey on the river Derwent and used for the same purpose until it became derelict some years later having been swept away in floods. It was then broken up by a Mr Lazenby.

The rivalry continued, but in any fishing community, care and help for one another whilst at sea always shines through. At 10 a.m. on 11 March 1888 a vessel was sighted trying to sail out of the Bay. The wind was east-south-east blowing a full gale with a flood tide. It was apparent to those onshore that the vessel would be wrecked. The National Boat was got ready as well as the *Seagull* and both lifeboats were taken to the North Beach. By this time the vessel was just outside the shore breakers with two anchors down. Both lifeboats launched and went to the vessel's aid; the *Seagull* was the first to get through the shore break and managed to rescue the crew of seven from the schooner *Impulse* of Ryde. The National Lifeboat, not being required, came

12. *Launching the* William John and Francis, *showing how the four horses with drivers were positioned. Two were harnessed to each side of the lifeboat carriage.*

ashore and was re-carriaged. Then the coxswain and crew waited on the beach, with the *William John and Frances*, until the *Seagull* lifeboat and her crew were safely back on shore. The vessel *Impulse* subsequently became a total wreck.

In September 1889, a newspaper article described the events of a normal exercise by the *Seagull* lifeboat:

> The rough sea combined with a strong easterly wind was an ideal time for an exercise with the popular lifeboat. The *Seagull* was taken to the beach where a splendid launch took place at full tide, with a crew of 14 and some passengers. All on board got a good wetting, before the boat got clear of the breakers. All the passengers seemed to enjoy the ducking they got, some of the breakers going completely over the lifeboat as she launched. The boat was then rowed to the front of the North Pier, riding amongst the breaking water like a beautiful bird from which she takes her name. To the enjoyment of those on the shore she was then rowed into the harbour where some of the crew exhibited the lifejackets they were wearing, which were made of cork, by jumping out of the boat into the harbour. Those who saw the *Seagull* afloat were well pleased with her performance. The committee of the Sailors and Working Men's Institute were at liberty to thank all those who assisted and contributed in any form to its upkeep.

In November 1889 a newspaper cutting reported how some funds were collected:

> We are requested by the committee of the Sailors and Working Men's Institute to thank Mr J. Pawson, Sea Breezes, for his special donations to the funds of the *Seagull* lifeboat. It appears Mr Pawson has a rule, that all visitors, who go in late, to the public dinner, are fined the sum of 1 penny and the money raised is given to the funds of this excellent lifeboat.

This way of raising funds for the Bridlington lifeboat still carries on today. Some guesthouse owners, on the firing of maroons to call the lifeboat crew to the boathouse, make a point of taking a collecting box round their visitors, thereby raising funds for the Bridlington lifeboat.

It was not every time that lifeboat men were called to duty that their strenuous efforts to save life succeeded, as was the case on 16 February 1890.

At daybreak a schooner was observed in difficulty three to four miles south of the harbour. There was a gale blowing from the east and signal rockets were fired at the National Society's lifeboat station to summon the lifeboat crew, who speedily turned out. At once they proceeded to Barmston lifeboat house, in order to launch the lifeboat stationed there. The volunteer life company were also quickly on the move with the life-saving apparatus, on board carts. On reaching the schooner, it was found that she had been abandoned previous to coming ashore. From the appearance of the vessel her crew must have left hurriedly, as all the sails were still set. The vessel's name was *Kate* of St Ives and she was carrying a cargo of coal.

It was supposed that she had sprung a leak and the crew, thinking she was sinking, had possibly been taken off by some passing vessel. With no life in danger, the Barmston lifeboat was not launched. It was highly probable that the stranded vessel was to become a total wreck.

The lifeboat crew and helpers from Bridlington had travelled four miles along the beach in bad weather; owing to the softness of the sand they had walked most of the way. The wagonettes and horses that had been hired to transport them to Barmston, were only useful on firm sand. On the return journey the men walked the whole way back to Bridlington, through the gale force wind and rain. Each of the 13 men who would have formed the crew of the lifeboat, had she been launched, for their efforts received five shillings (25p in today's currency). Nine men who would have assisted in launching the lifeboat also received five shillings. The hire of two wagonettes and horses, for transport of the crew and helpers, cost £2 10s. (£2.50 in today's currency).

The End of the 1800s

On 22 November 1890 an exercise was called for the national boat *William John and Frances* by the lifeboat inspector, Cdr Graham. As was the custom, to select the crew of the lifeboat for an exercise and also beach men, lots were drawn on the beach from a bag held by the coxswain. The men who formed the lifeboat crew were paid four shillings each, whilst the beach men who helped launch the boat received two shillings each. A position in the crew was the most sought-after on account of the extra money. As lots were drawn, the beach men became dissatisfied and requested the same pay as those who manned the boat, arguing that the work they did was the heaviest, dirtiest and wettest. The inspector said he could not alter the RNLI regulations, which were laid down by the institution. Therefore, the men declined to launch the boat and it was taken back to the boathouse without being exercised.

The same night a meeting was called to try to resolve the differences between the men. Cdr Graham met with the men, about 100 fishermen. Their spokesman said the two shillings the beach men will receive would have helped pay for the fuel to dry their clothes. They ran the greater risk of catching cold, being wet through launching the boat and then having to wait on the beach until the boat came back in again. In these circumstances they thought they were entitled to the same pay as the lifeboat crew. When the lifeboat was given money from salvage services, the beach men only got four shillings. Not long ago the lifeboat crew had received £5 each which was considered very unfair, as the beach men were also qualified to form the crew of the boat, which they would do if extra crew were required. The inspector replied that he would pass on their grievances to the institution. The fishermen unanimously resolved that this grievance only applied to exercises and there would be no hesitation on the part of the men, in carrying out their duties as usual in the event of life being at risk from shipwreck. Mr West, the Honorary Secretary, said he was unaware of the men's grievances and that he may resign. One week later, on 28 November, Mr West formally resigned at a meeting held in the Sailors and Working Men's Institute, Cliff Street. Mr West had approached Col Rickaby who had agreed to take up the now vacant post; Mr West added that if he hadn't found anybody so able to fill the post he would not have resigned. He also appealed for a better understanding between those responsible for the two lifeboats in the town. A little rivalry, he thought, was good, stating he thought the *Seagull* was the better lifeboat for the surf and that the national lifeboat was better for the offshore work. There had been many cases where both boats had launched to one vessel, increasing the cost without saving any more lives. His farewell message was that somehow genuine effort must be made to solve the problem, making both boats more efficient without undue rivalry.

The RNLI in 1898 brought in new rates, which were generally adopted throughout the service, and would in future be paid here to the crew on exercise and to the helpers on services and exercises. The crew would be paid for services in accordance with the regulations as heretofore.

Men already enrolled in the Brigade, or who wished to enrol, were desired to meet the Hon Secretary at the Sailors' and Working Men's Club on Saturday, 5 March 1898 at 3 p.m. for the purpose of giving their consent to this scale:

SCALE OF PAY AT BRIDLINGTON QUAY:
A BRIGADE OF 30 MEN TO BE ENROLLED

Exercise.	13 crew	5s summer	7s 6d winter	10s night
	16 helpers	3s summer	4s 6d winter	6s night exercise any time of year
	1 signalman			total men 30
Extra Pay.	3 Shaft Men	(1 shilling each extra, both summer, winter and night		
	1 Hook Rope Man)			
	6 Men who ride horses into water (2s 6d each on all occasions)			
Services	13 crew as per scale in regulations			
	16 Helpers (3s day service, summer 6s night service, summer 4s 6d intermediate, summer)			
	1 Signalman (4s 6d day service winter, night service, winter 6s 9d intermediate, winter)			

The SIGNALMAN is paid extra when he is kept an unusually long time on watch.

THOMAS ATKIN, Hon Sec

The Lifeboat Demonstration

During the following three-year period relationships certainly improved. On 7 July 1893 'The Great Lifeboat Demonstration' took place at Bridlington to raise funds for the

RNLI. Eight lifeboats, six life-saving companies and four bands all combined to make this a most colourful event and the finest Bridlington had seen for some years. More than 12,000 visitors flooded into the town to witness the spectacle and 24 rail excursions arrived that day from towns and cities such as Scarborough, York, Harrogate, Bradford, Dewsbury, Halifax, Sheffield and Hull.

The event commenced with a swimming and life-saving exhibition in the harbour by Leeds swimming club, followed by a water polo match and all the aquatic games. At midday the main parade passed along gaily decorated streets, headed by six mounted policemen from the East Riding Constabulary. Then came the 1st East Riding of Yorkshire Volunteer Artillery with four heavy guns, which later fired a Royal Salute. Following on came the Princes Parade band, members of the Bridlington local board in three carriages, the Hornsea Life-saving Company, and the Hornsea RNLI lifeboat, *Ellen and Margaret of Settle* manned by Coxswain White and his crew. Next came both Flamborough lifeboat crews wearing cork lifebelts. *Matther Middlewood* from South Landing and *Mary Frederick* from North Landing were not in the procession as they did not have lifeboat carriages, both being slipway launching boats.

They had been launched during the morning and rowed into Bridlington Bay where they took part in a water procession later in the day. Following the Flamborough lifeboat men in the parade were the Flamborough Life-saving Company. Then came the Filey RNLI lifeboat *Hollon II*, manned by Coxswain Wyville and his crew, her carriage pulled by eight horses. Then the 1st West Yorkshire Rifle Volunteer band followed by representatives of the Trade Societies, the Druids Friendly Society, the Ulrome Life-saving Company. The Barmston, RNLI lifeboat, *George and Jane Walker* with her crew, including Coxswain Purvis on board. Then came a number of the events organising committees, followed by the Hull Spring Bank Sailors Orphan band, and then HM. Coastguard. Next came the Bridlington Life-Saving Company preceded by the rocket apparatus wagon, hauled by four horses, the fishermen's lifeboat *Seagull*, looking smart after a new coat of white paint with Coxswain G. Wallis and her full crew on board. Following the *Seagull* were the two survivors of the lifeboat disaster of 1871, R. Hopper and R. Bedlington, who were warmly applauded along the route. Bringing up the rear of the procession was the 2nd Volunteer Brigade of the East Yorkshire Regiment with the band, followed by a model of Grace Darling and her father in a coble, the Bridlington RNLI lifeboat *William John and Frances*, with Coxswain R. Wallis and a full crew on board, then a display of model ships and lifeboats constructed by local man, Mr P. Anderson. At the end of this magnificent parade the lifeboat was taken on to the beach and launched into the Bay where they joined the Withernsea lifeboat and the two Flamborough lifeboats, which were riding at anchor. The magnificent sight of eight lifeboats in Bridlington Bay at one time had never been witnessed before or since. To complete the afternoon entertainment the Barmston crew demonstrated the self-righting capabilities of their lifeboat by capsizing her. Lieut. Young put the life-saving companies through their paces with the rocket apparatus. A very successful day concluded with a grand firework display, staged on the Princes Parade sea wall, during the evening.

On 18 November 1893, once again the area was swept by severe weather conditions – north-easterly hurricane-force winds, with heavy rain and hail showers. Many distress flares had been seen far out to sea during the night from Flamborough to Spurn, many ships were in distress and two vessels had become total wrecks in the Bay, but happily, thanks to services by the volunteer life-saving company and fishermen, their crews had been rescued. The *Pearl* of Goole had been on passage from London to Bridlington Quay, with a cargo of bones, when about three miles south of Bridlington harbour she had signalled for assistance. Four men had been taken out by a coble and put on board.

Later, with the weather worsening, a small ketch was seen to be drifting towards the shore, with all her sails blown away and flying signals of distress. The *William John and Frances* was launched at 10.00 a.m. and proceeded to the casualty 2½ miles south of Bridlington. Before she could be reached the *Pearl* of Goole was driven ashore, onto the beach, by the severe weather. On arriving at the scene the lifeboat attempted to get alongside to rescue the seven men on board. In trying to do so, the stress of wind combined with the heavy breaking swells that struck the lifeboat and she was driven high onto the beach. Because of the ebbing tide and lack of manpower they were unable to re-launch the lifeboat. By this time the rocket apparatus had arrived. The apparatus was set up, but because of the severity of the storm the first rocket line carried away downwind, missing its target completely. As quickly as was humanly possible, the men with cold, numb hands, set up a second rocket and fired, this time hitting the wreck. The crew attached a heavy rope to the rocket line, which was pulled ashore and used to bring the seven men on board the *Pearl* to safety.

The lifeboat must have been left on the beach overnight, the crew and helpers returning home to Bridlington. As we know, one of the crew on this lifeboat service, Richard Purvis, during the early morning of 19 November 1893, was to leave Bridlington harbour with four other men in the small coble *Swiftsure*, which belonged to Mr G. Champlin, to rescue the crew of the *Victoria* (see page 118). Not until 8.00 a.m. the next day did the lifeboat return to the lifeboat house in Bridlington. Great difficulty must have been encountered. It is reported that 12 horses were used to pull the lifeboat carriage across ploughed land, cart tracks and turnip fields and Coxswain Tallentire reported breaking a number of gateposts on the homeward journey.

On 20 November 1893, the lifeboat was called for again. At daylight a strong gale was still blowing from the east-north-east with a heavy sea. At 10.00 a.m. a steamer was observed flying the flag of distress from her foremast. Once again the *William John and Frances* was launched. Coxswain Tallentire had collapsed while assembling the crew: perhaps this had been put down to the exhausting struggle of the previous day's lifeboat service. The lifeboat was launched and proceeded to the steamer *Rayner*, on passage from the Tyne to Dublin with its cargo of coal. Despite the strong gale with heavy seas, the lifeboat managed to get alongside the steamer, then after some difficulty to get a man on board her to act as pilot. The anchor was slipped and the steamer moved into the Bay, getting a small lee from Flamborough Head. The steamer's cargo had shifted and her decks were awash in the bad weather, so she lost overboard the chief mate. Once again on board the lifeboat as a crewman was Richard Purvis. This was his third launch to rescue lives in three days.

Ill-feeling against RNLI officials again surfaced on 30 November 1897. During a violent gale the steamship *Bordeaux*, sank with the loss of her crew. At 3.00 a.m. a lighthouse keeper and a coastguard signalman at Flamborough saw a vessel on the rocks firing distress flares. The Flamborough No. 2 lifeboat, *Matthew Middlewood*, was launched from South Landing and proceeded to the aid of the stricken vessel, which by this time was drifting off towards the Smithic Sands. The casualty continuously sent out distress signals, which could be seen from Flamborough and Bridlington. After carefully considering the state of the sea and the direction of the wind, together with a position of the casualty, Captain Atkin, the Honorary Secretary of the Bridlington lifeboat, refused permission for the *William John and Frances* lifeboat to be launched.

The Flamborough lifeboat, after two valiant attempts, was unable to cross the Smithic Sands, across which a tremendous sea was running, so then returned to South Landing. On realising no help was going to be available, William Scales, owner of the fishing coble *Florence*, removed fishing gear and nets from the coble and with 12 volunteers, including Richard Purvis, left Bridlington harbour and went to the steam trawler *Magnetic* of Grimsby, which was anchored in the Bay, to explain what had happened. The trawler proceeded in the hope of picking up any survivors but on arrival in the area nothing could be seen but the two masts. The *Bordeaux* had sunk with all hands.

The lifeboat men had wanted to launch but it was Captain Atkin that prevented them going to the aid of the *Bordeaux*, once again causing friction, which boiled over one week later. On Monday, 13 December at 9.15 a.m. the coxswain informed the Honorary Secretary, Captain Atkin, that two fishing cobles were at sea wanting assistance. The wind was south-south-east force 7 to 8, causing heavy swell at the harbour mouth and making it dangerous for the open cobles to enter the harbour. Captain Atkin went to the boathouse and found a crowd of men at both front and back doors. He told the men at the back door to go to the front and take their chance of getting on the crew with the others, according to the custom. They refused to move. Captain Atkin said he wouldn't open the doors until the men did as he had asked and walked away. The men then seized a small mast lying nearby and broke down the back door. The lifeboat was then taken out of the boathouse and launched from the slipway of the South Pier, under the command of the coxswain. The lifeboat lay just off the harbour entrance until the two cobles had safely entered the harbour; the lifeboat was then taken back on to the North Beach for re-carriage and return to the boathouse. Captain Atkin said that afterwards he had every intention of allowing the lifeboat to launch had the men obeyed his orders. After consulting with the local committee and district inspector it was recommended that the crew and helpers be paid according to the scale of the institution.

At 11.00 p.m. on 13 December 1897, the coastguard contacted Captain Atkin asking for the lifeboat to be launched. There was a vessel ashore at Danes Dyke, requiring assistance. The wind was south-south-westerly with a strong breeze. The message was passed on to Coxswain Williamson who fired the maroons to call the men to the boathouse. Captain Atkin then returned to his bed. The lifeboat *William John and Frances* was taken to the North Beach. With no horses available, the crowd, which had assembled in response to the signal rocket, pulled the boat via Clough Bridge (Bridge Street) along the Promenade. Arriving just after midnight, they found the *Seagull* lifeboat had already launched, having seen the flares at 10.30 p.m. She had been taken from the Sailors Institute and pulled by hand along the Promenade to Trinity Cut, where she had been speedily launched, at about the same time a coble went to the grounded vessel. From the harbour also there were the Volunteer Life Company and a Flamborough coble. The captain of the *Toncoy*, of Dublin, on route from Dover to Sunderland in ballast, seeing that the tide was going out and that the ship was in no immediate danger declined any help, but did ask the *Seagull* and the Flamborough coble to stand by him for the night and the crew remained onboard.

An attempt was made to get the National Lifeboat afloat, but because of the softness of the sands and the refusal of the four farm horses, which had been acquired to launch the lifeboat into the water (work to which they were not accustomed), it was found impossible to drag the carriage far enough into the water to launch the lifeboat; eventually the boat was taken back onto the beach. While loading the launching equipment and ropes back into the lifeboat, the carriage wheels had sunk deep into the sand. Just as four more horses arrived, a message was received that the national boat was no longer required. The horses made several attempts to start the carriage moving, but the wheels were deeply embedded in the soft sand. The eight horses and people pulling on the drag ropes managed to free the carriage from the sand and get it moving. Feeling their load released, the horses pulled the carriage at speed towards the slipway. As they did so an elderly gentleman named Mr Rogers, a journalist, failed to get out of the way, was knocked down by one of the horses and run over by the offside wheel of the lifeboat carriage. Two doctors Godfrey and Forrest, who happened to be on the beach, attended the poor man but the accident had killed him instantly.

After the events of December 1897 feelings in the community must have been at an all-time high.

At 8 a.m. on the morning of 25 March 1898, a small ketch named *Beaconsfield*, which had been riding at anchor off the North Pier, was swept from her anchor during the east-north-east severe gale that was blowing. The vessel was driven towards the South Beach opposite Hilderthorpe Lodge (today the golf club). The tide was ebbing and she was driven right up to the cliff. Her movements had been watched from the shore, the rocket life-saving apparatus was quickly on the spot and the national lifeboat, *William John and Frances* was taken to the scene. The crew of the *Beaconsfield* decided in the circumstances with ebbing tide that they would not leave the vessel and the lifeboat stayed on the scene until the vessel had dried out. The lifeboat was then returned to the boathouse at 11.45 a.m.

Throughout the previous week the area once again had been the scene of violent storms, which continued with unabated fury throughout the day from the east-north-east force 9 to a hurricane, with blinding showers of hail and snow. The whole bay was a mass of white water and huge waves swept over the piers and sea wall with terrific force. The vessels which were riding out the gale at anchor in the north part of the Bay were watched by hundreds of spectators from the shore. Two vessels were seen to hoist small flags up their masts, which was taken by the fishermen to mean that the vessels needed assistance. The time was 6.00 p.m.: high tide.

Immediately, both the National lifeboat *William John and Frances* under the command of Coxswain James Williamson and the *Seagull* lifeboat were on the move. Captain Atkin had immediately agreed the use of the national boat, which was pulled across the town to the North Beach by six horses. The secretary of the Sailors and Working Men's Club together with the coxswain had gone to the cliff top to inspect the conditions. In their absence the *Seagull* was pulled by hand to Limekiln Lane slipway; the national boat was taken down Carr Lane (Sand's Lane) slipway. The older fishermen advised against launching at high tide with the heavy seas breaking on to the sea wall with such violence, as the vessels showing distress signals were not in imminent danger, and to wait an hour for the tide to ebb. Then, if it was not possible for the lifeboat to be rowed into the stormy sea, they would have some beach to return to with some degree of safety. The younger fishermen decided against waiting, possibly to show bravery under such conditions. Were they angry with the bureaucracy and rules and regulations, which were now in force, which were stopping them doing what they had always done? Or had the rivalry between the two lifeboat crews come to the surface once again? Thousands of spectators had gathered along the Alexandra Sea Wall and sea front to witness the lifeboat being launched. Had this played a part in the decision to launch the lifeboats?

The two lifeboats launched at about the same time. The spectators could clearly see that both lifeboat crews were unable to row against the heavy breakers, which were crashing against the lifeboats driven by the violence of the wind. The national boat, on launching from the slipway, encountered a serious problem; one of the four ropes holding the lifeboat onto the carriage was not released in time and a heavy sea struck the boat on the port bow, driving her towards the sea wall and washing the carriage off the slipway. The crew of the *Seagull* lifeboat were breaking oars in their strenuous efforts to row through the shore break, but were being driven back against the sea wall, pounded by the raging sea.

The crews of the two lifeboats were now battling for their own lives. The cheers of the crowd, on seeing the lifeboats launching, had turned to shouts of panic, with women screaming. The shout went up for ropes. As this was happening, the boats were being driven south along the sea wall. Men came running with ropes, which were thrown to the crewmen in the boats, one by one as the opportunity arose; they were dragged up the sea wall, battered and bruised but to safety. Some of those pulled from the lifeboats had broken limbs, others had cuts, and some were suffering from cold and exposure. One of the men helping to pull the lifeboat men to safety was Christopher (Kit) Brown. His son Fred was a crew member in the *Seagull* lifeboat. As she drifted along the sea wall 'Kit' went down the steps to help his son, who was still inside the battered lifeboat. A large wave hit 'Kit' and washed him into the sea. Fred managed to catch hold of him tying a rope around his father; he was then hauled up the sea wall. Nearing the top, the rope snapped and 'Kit' fell back into the boiling surf. Mr Stephenson, the harbour master, was lowered down the sea wall on a rope into the raging sea. He managed to catch hold of 'Kit' and together they were pulled up the sea wall, but Mr Stephenson was unable to hold on to 'Kit' who fell back into the sea. Mr Stephenson made a second descent into the sea, but becoming exhausted with the cold, was unable to hold on to 'Kit' who drifted away and was drowned.

By the time the lifeboats had been driven to Trinity Cut all the men had been pulled to safety. Considering the conditions it had been nothing short of a miracle. Robert Pickering, his leg badly broken, was taken to Lloyd's Cottage Hospital. William Jewitt, second coxswain of the *William John and Frances*, was taken home with back injuries; his son Jack Jewitt had been badly cut on the face. J.R. Hopper was another injured and Tom Clarke had cuts to the head. Very few of the men escaped without being bruised or cut and most suffered from some degree of exposure.

Both lifeboats were eventually washed up at Trinity Cut. The *Seagull* was a complete wreck, while the *John William and Frances* was unfit for further service.

Christopher (Kit) Brown was 56 years old; his body was washed up three days later at Hornsea, 12 miles along the coast.

A local fund was launched, to which the RNLI donated £25, for his widow and 11 children. He was given a naval funeral. His coffin draped in a union flag was carried from the bottom of Ship Hill, where he lived, to the hearse, which was waiting at the top of the hill, by six young apprentices, A. Charlton, W. Jewitt, F. Sawdon, J. Usher, F. Burdell and F. Walkington Senior. The apprentices represented his fellow workmen from Mr J. Rennard's building works, where he had been employed at the time of his death. The funeral cortège contained representatives from businesses throughout the town, as well as the lifeboats and fishing community. Many messages of condolence were sent from towns and villages throughout the land. At the committal it was said,

> We have today laid to rest, in the care of our God, a very brave man, who all his life has lived to help others, saving many from a watery grave. His motto was 'The sea shall not have them,' but alas he went once more on his errand of mercy and saved three valuable lives, and then at last, gave his own life to the sea while trying to save others.

One of the vessels that had caused the two lifeboats to launch was the *Lucinda*. She later tried to enter the harbour without the aid of a pilot, missing the entrance completely. She went aground on the South Beach, eventually being broken up. The volunteer rocket brigade and breeches buoy rescued all the crew.

During the same storm the North Smithic buoy was driven from its moorings washing ashore at Barmston. It took 12 horses to bring it back to Bridlington harbour. On the same tide a small boat bearing the name '*Annie*, Grimsby 496, Appleyard,' was washed ashore on the South Beach. It indicated that a fishing smack with all hands had been lost.

A special committee meeting was held on 6 April 1898 at the Sailors and Working Men's Club, after hearing the report, to decide what action to take with the wrecked *Seagull* lifeboat. After hearing a report on the events of that day, it was proposed that the committee should not undertake the responsibility of another lifeboat. It was proposed by Mr Johnson and seconded by Mr D. Walkington that the boat be place near Northcliffe (now the seaward end of Regent Terrace) on exhibition during the summer and the proceeds be given to the Lloyd's Cottage Hospital. The vote was carry unanimously.

One month later the RNLI committee of management in London wrote to Captain Atkin, local Honorary Secretary for the RNLI, informing him that the Institution had decided to close the Barmston lifeboat station, as they had decided that a lifeboat in that area was unnecessary. The Barmston lifeboat *George and Jane Walker* would be transferred to the Bridlington station to provide lifeboat cover until a permanent replacement for the *William John and Frances* could be built. The ex-Barmston lifeboat served at Bridlington until October 1899, without being called out on service. She was then sold out of service by the RNLI.

The *George and Jane Walker* had been stationed at Barmston and crewed from Bridlington for 14 years, during which time she had only been launched on service once, saving no lives. The *William John and Frances*, during the same period, was stationed at Bridlington for 13 years and launched on service a total of 16 times saving 44 lives.

13. *The* Seagull *Lifeboat after being wrecked in March 1898, outside its Boathouse, which was part of the Sailors and Working Men's Club in Cliff Street.*

At the Sailors and Working Men's Club a special general meeting was called on 7 September 1898. There was a good attendance, amongst those present being Mr J. Johnson, Capt. Atkin, Mr J. W. Postill, hon. sec., Mr C. Wardill, Messrs M. Walkington, F. Reed, F. Postill, G. Walkington and J. Whitehead. Mr Johnson was voted to the chair. The secretary explained to the meeting that, when the *Seagull* was brought into being, there was only one lifeboat station in the immediate area, the next one along the coast being at Hornsea. There were no lifeboats at Flamborough; Bridlington's lifeboat had been deemed unsuitable for the area, being too heavy. The Rev. Lloyd Greame had agreed to supply the fishermen with a lifeboat of their choice. In the 1870s sailing vessels were ten times as numerous as they were in the 1890s. The National Lifeboat Institution was now perfectly willing to allow men to select a type of lifeboat they could approve of, which was very different from the way boats were stationed on the coast in 1871. The secretary made it known, that two ladies had generously offered to supply a new lifeboat to the Sailors and Working Men's Club, if the club would take charge of it on their behalf. This kind offer had been declined, the secretary stating his reasons for doing so, with which the ladies were perfectly satisfied. During discussions, once again the care for each other came to the surface. The question put forward in support of a new lifeboat was, 'Suppose the National Boat went out and got into difficulties, and there was no other lifeboat to render assistance to the crew, lives might be in jeopardy. Do we stand on the shore and watch the men drown?' Captain Atkin, Honorary Secretary to the national boat, said in his opinion that the lifeboat stationed at Barmston was of little or no use. It had been stationed there for some 14 years and had not once been required to save life. Now that the lifeboats were able to sail rather than rely on manpower alone, if a boat was needed in the area at Barmston, Bridlington lifeboat could reach it with a northerly wind, and with a southerly wind the lifeboat from Hornsea would be available. With three lifeboats within 15 miles of each other it was decided that the club should not take management of another lifeboat.

At the AGM the following February, it was proposed by Mr Johnson and seconded by Mr Woodhouse that £167 13s. 2d., being the balance left in the '*Seagull* Lifeboat Fund', be given to the Lloyd's Cottage Hospital on condition that 'any sailor or fisherman who may accidentally be injured, when following his calling, be admitted to the hospital free, providing his age shall be 30 years or more'. This proposal was carried unanimously. The *Seagull* lifeboat house was to be used to enlarge the club's facilities.

Bridlington Branch of the National Lifeboat Institution

Statement of the receipts and expenditure
from 1 January 1899 to the 31 December 1899

Receipts				Expenditures				
January, 1899								
	£	s	d			£	s	d
Balance in hand	13	11	1	Jan. 13 Cash paid Williamson		4	0	0
Annual subscriptions and				17 Bailey's account		4	8	4
boat house collections	28	12	7	23 Advertising		0	10	6
Contribution box	6	15	5	27 Rates		1	11	7
Demonstration fund	9	6	8	Mar. 9 Sampson at boathouse		1	2	0
Circus company	5	16	8	April 3 Quarter's salary		3	10	0
Cash from parent Society	56	4	4	6 Mr. Jackson 1s, Cooper		9	10	0
	£120	6	9	6 Mr. Crowther's account				
				Painting and cleaning				
				boathouse		15	15	4
				June 4 Purvis, quarter's salary		2	10	0
				4 Tank cleaning		0	7	6
				4 Tipping plates cleaning		1	10	0
				4 Signalman and Bowman		0	12	6
				July 4 Printing		1	4	0
				15 Mr. Renards bill		3	5	5
				Oct. 3 Quarters salaries		3	10	0
				26 Exchanging boats		10	12	0
				Nov. 2 Practising boats		11	11	0
				3 Assemble crew, etc.		9	10	0
				Dec. 5 Printers bill		0	8	6
				15 Mr. Renards bill		7	19	0
				18 Blacksmith's bill		0	4	0
				18 Bag for pillar box		0	2	0
				18 Brushes		0	2	0
				18 Stores from London		0	18	6
				18 Quarterly Salaries		3	10	0
				18 Postage and Police		1	2	6
				BALANCE		31	0	1
						£120	6	9

Notice. The annual general meeting of the subscribers of the above institution will be held in the Sailors and Working Men's Club, Cliff Street, Bridlington, on Tuesday next, 27 Mar 1900, at three o'clock.

The Hon. Secretary begs to remind subscribers to the institution that their subscriptions are now due.

THOS. ATKIN Hon. Sec.

4

The *George and Jane Walker*

The events of 1898 seem to have been a catalyst to bring the community together. They had been trying so hard in so many individual ways to prove they had the capabilities and skills to save life at sea, without realising that they were all trying to do the same thing. With so many available lifeboats it was easy for friction to be created between them. Added to that was the need to earn money to feed the family, as they had done with the *Harbinger* lifeboat, using it both as a pilot boat and for supplying necessary provisions for the many sailing ships anchored in the Bay, or as a crew-member of the national lifeboat receiving a small cash reward, or from salvage money paid by the owners of the ships they helped.

The coastal trade on which Bridlington had relied was now only a trickle. By contrast, the fishing industry had increased and the improved harbour facilities attracted fishermen and their boats to Bridlington, from Flamborough and Hornsea and as far away as Norfolk. They could also transport the catch to better markets inland by train. In periods of poor fishing the fishermen found other ways to earn a living, turning to the holidaymakers who now came to the seaside by train, and taking visitors for boat trips in the Bay. With the coming of the railway, Bridlington itself had changed from two small separate villages and had grown into a seaside town.

Since 1805 Bridlington lifeboat had always been taken to the site of the wreck on its carriage, pulled by horses or manpower, whether it had been on the North or South Beach. The lifeboat was then launched as close to the wreck as possible and the lifeboat men would row off to the wreck to carry out the rescue. This was the reason why the early lifeboat designs, similar to the ones built by Greathead, were 'double ended'. It allowed the boats to be rowed off the beach to the wreck, carry out the rescue, and then, without turning the boat round, which would have put the boat broadside on and vulnerable to storm-force breaking seas, the lifeboat could then row safely back to the beach. It was nearly impossible to row any distance in bad weather; the crew, exposed to the elements in what was an open rowing boat, quickly tired and suffered from exposure. If the wreck was to the north on the rocks towards Flamborough Head, the lifeboat was launched from the North Beach and rowed across the Bay. Men on horseback often reported vessels that were driven ashore along the Holderness coastline and could be seen from the land, by riding to Bridlington to pass the news to the coastguards and lifeboat. The lifeboat on its carriage would be taken to the site of the wreck as quickly as possible, taking into account the cart tracks and fields they had travelled along. If the vessels foundered at sea, out of the sight of land or another ship, the crew might disappear without trace.

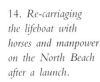

14. Re-carriaging the lifeboat with horses and manpower on the North Beach after a launch.

The *William John and Frances* class of lifeboats were proving that lifeboats fitted with sails now had the power to effect rescues further out to sea and at the greater distances along the shore.

By the late 1800s the RNLI understood that different lifeboat designs were needed to accommodate the different tasks that lifeboats around the coast of the British Isles were being called on to undertake. As a direct result of this Captain Atkin, the Honorary Secretary of the Bridlington RNLI, and a committee of local fishermen made a tour of the coast to see for themselves what class of lifeboat was likely to be the best suited for the conditions of Bridlington Bay, before the new lifeboat was built. From the information they supplied to the RNLI, a new lifeboat was specially built for the station at the Thames Iron Works, Blackwall, London.

The new lifeboat arrived at Bridlington on 23 October 1899. She was given the same name of the old Barmston lifeboat, *George and Jane Walker*, but a different RNLI official number (O.N.433). The cost of building her was £733, which came from the same £3,100 legacy left by Mr George Walker of Southport, from which the Barmston station had been financed earlier. The RNLI was now increasing the beam of the RNLI's self-righting lifeboats because the narrow-beamed boats had not found favour with the crews, as had been the case at Bridlington with the *John Abbott* lifeboat. The new lifeboat was larger than the *William John and Frances* that had been wrecked on the North Beach. Her design included many refinements drawn from almost half a century of development by the RNLI of the self-righting lifeboat. She weighed 3.6 tonnes, was 35 feet long, 8 feet 6 inches beam, and her crew consisted of a coxswain, second coxswain, bowman and 10 oarsmen. The first sea trials took place on 2 November 1899.

The new breed of cargo boat, built of iron and fitted with engines, which still travelled along the coast, was not at the sole mercy of the weather as were the coastal sailing ships, but the weather still did take its toll on some, as it still does today on the modern ship.

During thick fog in February 1900 the steamer *Dreaver*, on passage from Le Havre to North Shields, ran onto the rocks between South Landing and Flamborough Head. Being in ballast (without any cargo onboard), the sea pushed her nearly to the cliff.

15. *Horses pulling the lifeboat on carriage showing how it was transported to the site of wrecks along the coast.*

The vessel became embedded in the shore and resisted all efforts to pull her off. The owners of the vessel employed 30 fishermen, to excavate the chalk from around the vessel, and by the end of April she was towed off with little damage. Ironically 'Drever Dock', the area of excavation as the local fishermen know it, was the site from which the Bridlington lifeboat pulled the MFV *Normanby* on 6 January 1967.

On 15 November 1900 Bridlington Bay was swept by a south-westerly gale, accompanied by driving rain. The coastguards reported a vessel ashore near Auburn house, four miles south of Bridlington. The fishermen rushed to the lifeboat house all eager to get a lifebelt. The life-saving company, coastguards and a group of fishermen with a horse and cart, onto which they had loaded a coble, all hurried to Auburn. The lifeboat progress was slow; the route to Auburn, due to high spring tides covering the beach right up to the cliff, was through fields and fences. Much damage was done in turnip fields and along the way. The value of the damage would equal that of a pair of the six stout horses that were yoked up to the heaving lifeboat carriage, which sank constantly in the mire and clay on this strange route; in the end, they arrived at the scene about one and a half hours after the signal rockets had been fired. It seemed a long time, but it was a big effort and not a moment had been lost. The vessel was the *Jantje*, only six months old, an iron-built brigantine bound from Aberdeen to Hull with a cargo of granite. She had a crew of six. At about 10 o'clock her rudder had broken and with the rising tide she was helpless. The life-saving company fired a rocket with a line attached which was made fast to the vessel. The crew of the *Jantje* did not understand the workings of the rocket apparatus, even though the instructions had been sent onboard. With some difficulty the fishermen managed to get their coble alongside the vessel and persuaded the captain's two sons, William and Henry Ellison, to put on lifebelts and then to be taken ashore safely in the small coble. Once on the shore they were taken to Mr Hyde's farmhouse where they were treated in a very hospitable manner. The weather by this time was moderating, so the rest of the crew decided to stay on board the vessel, which was now in less danger. As all the crew were safe, the lifeboat was not required and made her way back to Bridlington along the beach to the slipway at the New Burlington Estate, just south of the harbour. The *Jantje*, was towed off the beach on the next tide by a tug and taken safely to Hull.

Towards the end of 1901 launching the lifeboat down Limekiln Lane 'Cut' was becoming difficult, due to the narrowness of the slipway. On 29 November 1901 the secretary of the lifeboat station, Captain

16. *The lifeboat* George and Jane Walker *under sail in the south part of the harbour.*

Thomas Atkin, wrote to the Town Clerk, Mr A. E. Matthewman, asking if it was possible for the Council to widen Limekiln Lane 'Cut' in order to accommodate the lifeboat. The Council through the Town Clerk then had to write to Lloyd Greame Esq JP of Sewerby House, asking his permission to carry out this work. The borough surveyor found the cut varied in width from 11 feet 6 inches to 14 feet, so in order to make it a uniform width of 15 feet the widening of the cut would have to be carried out on the Sewerby Estate side of the slipway. The dividing line for each property ran directly down the centre of the cut. Both parties agreed to the widening, and, after the work was completed, the slipway provided a safer and quicker launch site for the lifeboat.

The first record of the *George and Jane Walker* saving lives was on 14 December 1901. At 7 p.m. the coxswain observed a white light coming up the Bay. Shortly afterwards the vessel was showing distress flares. A heavy easterly gale was blowing with heavy seas and thick rainsqualls. The lifeboat was launched into the harbour, as it was nearing high tide and proceeded out of the harbour under sail, through a very heavy sea, under the command of Coxswain Richard Purvis. It sailed to the small ketch *Onward* of Montrose, which was on passage from Montrose to Portsmouth with a cargo of 80 tonnes of potatoes. The anchor was now dragging badly and the men on board the casualty had lit a second and third distress flare, illuminating the *Onward's* deck. From the shore the *George and Jane Walker* could be seen to go alongside with great difficulty and then they succeeded in taking off the four crewmen. Ten minutes after the rescue took place the ship was being dashed to pieces on the rocks between the North Pier and Princess Parade seawall. The lifeboat landed the four survivors safely in the harbour. On his return to the boathouse Richard Purvis was asked how the boat handled. He summed it up in one word, 'Splendidly'.

A telegram was sent to the postmaster at Montrose informing him that the crew of this vessel were safe and they would be obliged if the families were informed. On 16 December a reply came:

> We beg to thank you for your care and consideration in sending the telegram on Saturday night regarding the wreck of the *Onward*. Knowing that stormy weather was prevailing along the coast we were very anxious regarding the *Onward* and appreciate very highly the lifeboat's efforts.

Two years later the *George and Jane Walker* was to be tested again. On 9 December 1903, a south-south-easterly storm-force gale was blowing, with a very heavy sea and broken water. The coastguards had received information that a vessel was in difficulties to the south of Bridlington. A small ketch, the *Jehovah Jireh*, carrying salted herrings from Yarmouth to South Shields, came into view through a break in the weather, two miles from the shore and with only a small sail set. Seeing that the vessel would drift into danger Coxswain Richard Purvis fired the maroons to alert lifeboat crew. Without waiting for the horses to arrive, the boat was pulled by hand to Trinity Cut and onto the beach. The *George and Jane Walker* launched at 12.45 p.m., proceeding under sail to the casualty. A large crowd on the shore watched her progress and it was said that the fine boat showed her excellent sailing qualities to great advantage, making her way though the heavy seas that at times almost buried her. To avoid being driven on to the rocks of Flamborough Head the ketch had dropped an anchor, but almost immediately the anchor cable parted and she was driven on to the rocks scar, just to the East of Danes Dyke. Whitewater surrounded the stranded vessel. With first-class seamanship the lifeboat was taken to the Leeward of the vessel. Dropping their kedge anchor and after several attempts to get alongside, one by one the four crew of the stranded ship were taken off by the lifeboat. On its return journey at times it was obscured from the view of those watching from the seafront by the waves crashing over it.

Once again, when Richard Purvis was asked, how did the boat behave, he once again gave a one word in reply, 'Splendidly'.

In the years around the turn of the century many changes took place in the lifeboat service at Bridlington: 1899 saw the arrival of the new lifeboat the *George and Jane Walker*; in 1901 the town council acquired the site on which the lifeboat house was built, on the corner of Windsor Crescent and South Cliff Road, for street improvements. With the lease on the land running out, the RNLI decided that the cheapest option was to secure a new site for the lifeboat house, in order to pre-empt any future development of the land adjoining the present site. With this in mind enquiries were made about appropriate plots of land, prices and suitability for use as a lifeboat station in the close locality. A suitable plot was secured near Marine Drive. An advert in the paper invited contractors to tender for the construction of a brick and stone lifeboat house upon the site. In 1903 the new lifeboat house was built in South Marine Drive at a cost of £1211 15s. 9d. On 8 April 1904 it was reported that the lifeboat had moved to its new home.

This boathouse is still in use today. In 1979 a public appeal was made by Dr Terry Wilson, chairman of the Bridlington branch, for donations, which enabled a small extension to the side of the boathouse to be built. This provided heated changing rooms where the crew's oilskins and jumpers could be kept and a crew room in place of the old sail loft. On the front of this extension was built a small souvenir shop.

The *George and Jane Walker* lifeboat had gained the full respect of the whole fishing community; this boat was fully supported by the fishermen who agreed she was correctly constructed to face any weather conditions that might be encountered in Bridlington Bay. Anyone of them would have been proud to serve in her as a crew-member.

The *George and Jane Walker* again showed her fine qualities when on 22 December 1909 the lifeboat was called out to what was to become one of the last rescues from a wooden sailing ship, to be undertaken by a Bridlington lifeboat. The wind was blowing with hurricane force from the east–south-east with a heavy breaking sea right across the Bay. The brigantine *Guide of Leith* was on passage from Gravesend to Sunderland with a 300-ton cargo of chalk. At 8.30 a.m. she was seen one mile from shore with her sails in tatters. The crew of the casualty, seeing that they were in danger of being blown into the cliffs at Sewerby, managed to put out anchors which stopped their progress, bringing her up head to sea. At 9.00 a.m. Coxswain Richard Purvis fired the signal rockets to alert the lifeboat crew and as quickly as possible the boat was pulled to Trinity Cut by 150 pairs of willing hands before the horses arrived. At Trinity Cut she was launched into the water and immediately pounded by two or three large breaking waves. She behaved splendidly, sailing under the capable handling of Coxswain Purvis, ploughing into the angry seas and hidden in the troughs of the waves. Men from the lifeboat were put on board the casualty to help secure the anchors, after which all the crewmen from the *Guide of Leith* were taken into the lifeboat. Being high tide and with very little beach to return to, the lifeboat set sail to the harbour where the survivors, seven men and the dog owned by the captain, were landed safely and taken to the *Parade Hotel* where warm clothes and hot meals were waiting. The rescue had been witnessed by hundreds of people lining the seafront; a great cheer went up as the lifeboat sailed through the confused sea and safely into harbour.

The Hornsea Lifeboat

For some months the question of being able to raise sufficient men to crew the Hornsea lifeboat had been a very crucial matter within the small town. In December 1910 an inquiry was held in Hornsea about the continuation of the Hornsea lifeboat station. Insufficient numbers of volunteers were available, willing to offer their services to make up the lifeboat crew. At the inquiry it was decided to close the station and disband the few crew-members that were still available.

This news travelled to Bridlington, where men made it known to the RNLI that they were offering to take charge of it and crew the lifeboat at Hornsea, as they had done with the Barmston lifeboat some years earlier. On hearing this and knowing that there was, at that time, a need for a lifeboat at Hornsea, the decision by the RNLI to close the station was reversed.

The first practice took place on 14 January 1911. Mr F. Tallentire had been voted by the crew to be appointed coxswain and Mr E. Crawford second coxswain and together with six other men they assembled at the Central Garage, Prospect Street together with Lieut. Basil Hall, Lifeboat Inspector, Mr Parnell, Hon. Secretary for Bridlington lifeboat station and Capt. Redhead. They left Bridlington in what was described as three powerful cars, to make the 17½-mile journey to Hornsea. On reaching Hornsea they were joined by Mr C. Smith and four other volunteers who had been members of the old Hornsea crew. Within a short time the lifeboat *Ellen and Margaret of Settle* launched on a practice exercise. After the exercise the whole party from Bridlington was entertained to tea by the Hornsea lifeboat committee. The district inspector of lifeboats, Lieut. Basil Hall, announced that the exercise had been most successful and he was satisfied with the 63 minutes it had taken from the moment the cars had left Bridlington to the time the Hornsea lifeboat was launched. Volunteers from Bridlington had the unique distinction of providing the crew for the lifeboat in another town. This continued until the station eventually closed on 17 January 1924.

The *George and Jane Walker* adapted well to the change of use the lifeboats now encountered; more flexibility due to sailing a good, well-liked boat. The fishermen and community supported the one Bridlington lifeboat, the RNLI lifeboat.

The RNLI had to pay for the use of horses and also the special leather harness required by the horses when on lifeboat duty. As the lifeboat account from Mr. Cooper, Saddler and Harness maker, Queen Street, shows:

28th October 1912 New lifeboat belly-band 2 shillings 6 pence
New double leather girth 3 shillings
Spring hook and fitting 6 pence
6 Shillings paid 13th January 1913.
18th September 1913 New strap and buckle to girth 9 pence
New double lined girth 3 shillings
3 shillings 9 pence paid 5th January 1914.
19th June 1914 New extra long name strap fixing and oiling 1 shilling 9 pence paid 9th July
    1915.
25th February 1916 4 new horse collars. For use of corporation horses when transporting the
    Lifeboat carriage
£5 10 shillings paid 8th July 1916.

The fishing fleet, which consisted of open sailing cobles, sailed in the early morning of 29 November 1912 for the cod fishing grounds off Hornsea. The weather had changed during the morning with the wind strengthening from the west to a full gale. By midday concern was shown at the harbour for the 20 fishermen in the five cobles, working their lines at Hornsea as the wind continue to strengthen. The *George and Jane Walker* was launched 25 minutes after the alarm was raised, and with Coxswain Dick Purvis in command they sailed south. The cobles were all sailing together under storm sail off Ulrome. The cobles, *Three Brothers*, *Spray*, *Shamrock*, *Yorkshire Lass* and *Friends*, all had difficulty in sailing back into the harbour across the 'Canch' (the sand bar at the harbour entrance). Onlookers described the lifeboat as being 'beautifully handled', dodging about and cutting across the stern of each coble as she struck the cross seas of the harbour mouth. As each coble, buffeted by the waves, entered the harbour safely the *George and Jane Walker* tacked and lay awaiting the next boat; she behaved splendidly. It was watched by the fishermen's wives, who had joined the crowd of anxious spectators along the harbour walls. As the fishing industry in Bridlington increased for the next century the lifeboat's main work was giving aid to and saving lives within the fishing industry.

The First World War

The outbreak of war increased the dangers for the lifeboat crew. The danger to the community was compounded by the naval bombardment of Scarborough and Hartlepool by German naval vessels. On 16 December 1914, following these events, when the signal rockets to call the lifeboat crew to the boat house were fired, the inhabitants of Bridlington Quay asked, 'Is it the Germans or the zeppelins?' It was also known that

German submarines were patrolling off the Yorkshire coast. On 20 November 1914 Bridlington fishermen onboard the *Good Hope* reported that a German submarine was seen to be taking on petrol from a trawler off Flamborough Head. Fishing boats had been boarded, the fishermen were taken on board the submarines, and then the fishing boats were sunk.

On returning to Bridlington harbour on Friday, 19 May 1916 skipper Jacob Martin of the local fishing boat *Osprey* together with his crew spoke of a polite and humane German U-boat commander. As they were fishing off Bridlington, just out of sight of land, the U-boat appeared and ordered the fishing boat to go alongside. The crew of the fishing boat were then ordered onboard the submarine, which was only just level with the water, ready to dive at any moment. The U-boat commander chatted to them in very good English. Jacob said he hoped they were not going to take him and his crew prisoners. The German smilingly assured the fishermen that was not his intentions, nor did he want to drown anybody if he could help it. But he did have orders to sink all the fishing boats he could, which included the *Osprey*. The Germans gave the fishermen cigarettes and matches and not to be outdone skipper Martin offered the U-boat commander fish which he accepted politely.

The fishermen were onboard the U-boat for about half an hour, chatting. The U-boat commander shook hands with the fishermen before putting them into the fishing boat's *cauf* (a small rowing boat carried on the deck of each large fishing boat) and giving them directions to the nearest English ship. After rowing for some time they caught sight of the fishing boat *Busy Bee* which picked up the fishermen and return them safely ashore.

The Harbour Master Mr Harry Jackson received an order from the Admiralty to extinguish all lights under his control. The Admiralty also requested municipal authorities to reduce as much as possible the number of powerful electric lights on seafronts, esplanades and public places which are visible from the sea or from the air.

On the 18 March 1915 at 10.50 p.m. flares were seen in the Bay 2½ miles south of Bridlington. The signal rockets to call the crew were fired and without horses the lifeboat was pulled along the South Beach leaving the horses to follow. Also helping to pull the lifeboat were soldiers billeted in the town. The vessel in distress, a converted trawler, *Lord Airedale*, number 847, that had been mine sweeping for the Navy, was aground two miles south of Bridlington. The horses arrived at the same time and were hitched up to the lifeboat carriage, and they proceeded to launch the lifeboat into the sea. There were two horses on either side, as normal, with the riders Robert Carr, Tom Lakes, Charles Pashby and a volunteer from the crowd, Robert Brown. It was low water so the horses had to pull the carriage a long way into the breaking seas to enable the lifeboat to be launched. The first attempt failed. The launching falls had to be lengthened to allow the beach men, already up to the waist in water, to help pull the lifeboat off the carriage in the usual manner. A second effort was made to launch the lifeboat, but before this could happen the sea overwhelmed the lifeboat, which was still on the carriage, and washed her and her crew sideways off the carriage, smashing completely the large main carriage wheel. The sea also swept the horses off their feet and riders from the horses' backs. One of the riders, Robert Brown, was pulled from the sea into the lifeboat, another rider became entangled in the harness, unable to free himself or his horse from the lifeboat carriage, and Robert Carr was

17. *Launching the George and Jane Walker with horses. Note the two men on the left steering the carriage.*

drowned. Having been washed clear of the carriage by the seas, the lifeboat proceeded with great difficulty to the wreck. The hurricane-force wind drove the lifeboat before the seas and it passed the vessel without making contact. Despite valiantly attempting to get back to the wreck, they were driven onshore three-quarters of a mile to the south of the wreck. While this was happening, out of sight from those on the beach due to the weather conditions, the beach party were unable to pull the carriage back onto the beach. Fear and apprehension was felt by those onshore – faint cries had occasionally been heard above the howling wind. The efforts of the soldiers from the Norfolk regiment had been so great, trying to pull the carriage out of the sea back to the beach, that the ropes snapped. One horse rider, who had managed to free his horse from the carriage harness, appeared through the incoming breaking waves. The lack of a carriage to use, combined with the ferocity of the weather on the flood tide, made relaunching the lifeboat impossible. Helpless to do any further, work the lifeboat crew and helpers were forced to leave the *George and Jane Walker* on the beach. At 8 a.m. they trudged home exhausted through the blizzard. Returning after hot food and a change of clothing to secure the lifeboat, they tried at low water to recover the lifeboat carriage, which was buried in sand on the low-water mark. The main carriage axle had been broken when it was struck by a huge breaking sea which also broke one of the main wheels. One horse had been drowned but was still attached by its harness to the carriage. All 12 crew of the minesweeper 847 were drowned. The lifeboat was re-floated and taken back to the harbour where it remained until a new carriage could be sent to Bridlington by the RNLI.

A witness recalls:

> I was stationed at Bridlington with the battalion of the Norfolk regiment, where we were on coast defence duties which consisted of patrolling the cliffs at night, guarding the harbour and ship spotting. The night in question I was on patrol at Barmston when I saw distress signals being fired by a ship in Bridlington Bay. A minesweeper had taken refuge in the Bay; the storm force wind and heavy sea caused it to drag its anchor and it was being driven onshore. It was completely dark; no lights were allowed because of the blackout orders. The signal rockets sounded for the lifeboat crew; the fishermen pulled it along the beach with soldiers helping and later the horses joined them. I had seen the launching of the lifeboat before. The horses would enter the sea until the depth of water was sufficient for the lifeboat to float. Then the

horses on the left would turn left towards the shore, the rider would then release the harness leaving the carriage where it was until low tide when it was retrieved, the same procedure was taken by the men on the right-hand side horses. Unfortunately a huge wave caught the lifeboat capsizing it onto the right-hand horseman who was swept off his horse into the sea and was drowned. The horse got its legs trapped between the spokes of the wooden wheels of the carriage and was also drowned. Later the lifeboat was thrown onto a patch of sand under the cliffs by the high tide. The rocket apparatus could not be used because of the intensity of the storm that was blowing off the sea. The minesweeper was driven towards the cliff and eventually grounded and turned over. When daylight came I and a pal went to the beach again. I shall never forget the sight that met my eyes: men, blankets, ships' flags and other wreckage was strewn over the beach all left by the receding tide, the aftermath of that terrible night. Our battalion headquarters arranged horses and carts from the village pub. On our return to the beach, one by one the bodies of the minesweeper's crew were retrieved. Later identification and bodies were handed over to the Admiralty under whom they had been serving. I will never forget that night when those gallant men died for their king and country.

B.W. Chenery.

The First Bridlington Lifeboat Tractor

The First World War saw great advances in technology. In the years that followed the Great War, this technology filtered into everyday life allowing progress to be made in many fields. The lifeboat service was able to stride ahead with modernisation. The one project that was to help Bridlington lifeboat station was the development of the Caterpillar motor tractor, which was to replace the horses used to launch the lifeboat. Obtaining horses had become much more difficult. They had to be brought from farms on the outskirts of town, the nearest being Flat Top Farm on Kingston Road. As early as February 1913 the lifeboat committee had been forced to send a letter to the Town Clerk requesting the Corporation to provide 10 horses for hauling the lifeboat when required, as at that time only two horses were available from local farms. The letter pointed out the importance of the lifeboat at Bridlington which should be fully equipped, and ready for use at all times. The request was agreed to on the understanding that the RNLI paid a reasonable price for the hire of horses and drivers, and that all risk was fully covered by insurance. During the working day Corporation horses that were about the town were used; outside that time the horses were kept in fields on Fondbrig Lane (Wold Gate). Waiting for horses to arrive caused long delays in launching, together with increased costs to the RNLI for the hire of these horses. The Council minutes for 1917/18 give the charge for the service of Council horses to launch the lifeboat as £12. For some time the Institute had been looking for a faster way to launch lifeboats that relied on the carriage to take them to the water's edge. The tractor had proved itself both in war and now in agriculture. In December 1920 Bridlington lifeboat station was informed that tractors were being adapted to meet the requirements of the institution prior to being used around the coast. They were to arrange for the housing of such a tractor at Bridlington. The advert for the post of tractor driver appeared in the local paper. Thirty applicants: for the position of motor mechanic and driver of the new lifeboat tractor were later considered, together with several applications for the post of assistant. Mr Percy Hoggard was appointed driver, and Mr Albert Hutchinson assistant.

18. *Launching trials with the first lifeboat tractor in 1921.*

On 18 July 1921 trials were held in Bridlington of a 35hp Clayton Caterpillar tractor. It pulled the lifeboat and carriage from the lifeboat house on South Marine Drive across the town to launch at Trinity Cut. At the water's edge the tractor quickly moved to the other end of the carriage pushing the boat and carriage into the water. As a result of these first successful trials the RNLI modified the tractors they purchased to suit the conditions experienced while launching lifeboats.

The second trials were held on 25 March 1922. Officials and Heads of Department from the RNLI were assembled at the lifeboat house and at 6 p.m. the rockets were fired to call the crew. In only four minutes the *George and Jane Walker* was moving to Trinity Cut where it arrived in only ten minutes, less than half the time it had taken in the past with horses or when being pulled by hand. They encountered problems when the tractor skidded as it negotiated the cobblestones on the slipway down to the beach. A special tow bar had been fitted to the lifeboat carriage, which hooked onto the back of the tractor to enable the boat and carriage to be pulled down to the water's edge. The lifeboat pointing bow into the sea, and the tractor facing the sea wall, the tractor detaches from the carriage, and turns round ready to push the carriage into the water. The launching falls (ropes) are hooked onto the tractor. The carriage and boat are then pushed into the water, until there is sufficient depth of water for the lifeboat to be launched. At a signal from the coxswain, the ropes which fasten the lifeboat to the carriage are cast off, and at this point the tractor moves backwards out of the sea. The boat is propelled forward into the water and launched through the actions of the tractor, pulling backwards on the launching falls which pass round pulleys on the carriage.

A splendid launch was executed by Coxswain Hopper; also on board was Bridlington man Ernest Welburn, coxswain of the Hornsea lifeboat. After the exercise the lifeboat was re-carriaged. Again the steel plates on the tractor tracks caused problems by slipping on the slipway, but once these were overcome the lifeboat was taken back to the lifeboat house in South Marine Drive. The motor tractor proved its worth, taking 20 minutes off the time needed to launch the lifeboat. The tractor easily and efficiently was now doing the dangerous, wet, and cold job that the beach crew and horses had performed for 117 years.

On 17 November 1923 the fishing fleet sailed on a comparatively calm day, following a period of gale-force winds and bad weather. All remained well until 10.30 a.m. when the wind freshened and a heavy gale blew from the south-south-east. Most of the larger fishing boats had returned to harbour, but the sea increased as the wind strengthened even further into a violent storm. At 11.20 a.m. the lifeboat was launched from Trinity Cut, with Coxswain Hopper at the helm. As they were about to launch a huge breaking wave swept over the tractor stopping her engine dead. Men rushed into the sea fastening ropes to the carriage and with the help of spectators on the shore they managed to launch the lifeboat from the carriage into the sea. On clearing the carriage that lifeboat managed to sail and take a position off the harbour entrance as the open cobles fought their way into harbour against a violent sea. On approaching the harbour entrance, the 28-foot coble *Arrow* started shipping water from the waves breaking over her stern. The weight of water she had taken onboard pushed her broadside onto the swell, and then within 20 feet of the North Pier she sank. Seeing this the lifeboat ran in towards the wreck, which was being pounded by the heavy sea against the North Pier wall. The crew had been cast into the water;

19. *The first lifeboat tractor at Bridlington, March 1922.*

before the lifeboat was able to get to them the hurricane force winds had washed the wreck and crew to the north out of reach of the lifeboat. Five oars were broken in an effort to reach the men in the water, who were friends and neighbours of the lifeboat crew; the lifeboat was then driven back onto the beach. The rocket brigade was on the pier and made attempts to rescue the fishermen without success. Mr Stanley Willis, a local sail maker, volunteered to be lowered over the pier wall into the sea by means of a rope. On entering the water he managed to tie a rope around one of the fishermen, Sam Clark, who was unconscious, who was then pulled up onto the pier by the onlookers. During the operation a fur coat was put under the rope by Rear Admiral Sir Guy Gaunt, to prevent the rope fraying on the stone edge of the pier wall. Unfortunately Mr Clark had drowned. His body was placed on a stretcher and covered with the union flag, before being transported to his home.

The tractor on the beach had become completely unusable so a message was sent to the farms for horses. On their arrival on the beach, they were joined by a steam wagon, which was used to pull the lifeboat carriage out of the sand in which it had become embedded. The lifeboat was re-carriaged, after which the exhausted crew took her back to the boathouse. The bodies of the two other crew members of the *Arrow*, Fred Charlton and John Jack Pockley, where recovered on the North Beach days later.

Witnesses of this tragic event claim that a lifeboat with an engine may have prevented such a loss of life. No blame was attached to anyone; it had been the day when the wind and the sea combined to defeat every effort of man.

The *Arrow* was only five months old, built by local boat builders Mr Baker Siddall and his son Percy for Mr John G. Simpson, who had christened her *Elsie May*. The 39-foot coble had been specially designed for pleasure parties and fishing. She had changed her owners and, worse, her name; locally to change a fishing boat's name is thought to be unlucky.

At a meeting of the committee of management of the Royal National Lifeboat Institution for the Preservation of Life from Shipwreck, held at the London offices, on 20 December 1923, the following minute was ordered to be recorded in the book of the Society: that the best thanks of the Royal National Lifeboat Institution be presented to Harry Hopper, coxswain of the Bridlington lifeboat, in recognition of his skilful seamanship and fine efforts, when he and the crew of the lifeboat attempted to rescue the crew of the fishing boat *Arrow* which was totally wrecked off Bridlington harbour during an exceptionally heavy southerly storm with a very heavy sea, 15 November 1923.

In 1928 an extension to the sea wall, which protected the Spa Royal Hall and Theatre, was built, extending south 2,750 feet. It was built 80 feet out from the cliffs, and by doing this reclaimed the land from the sea. A slipway was built from this promenade up to the road level. This was to enable easy access to the South Beach for launching the lifeboat. The area was called Princess Mary Promenade and was opened by the Princess on 7 September 1928.

This slipway is still known locally as Levitt's Hill after the builders who carried out this work, Messrs Levitt Ltd of Hull and Hornsea.

5

The First Motor Lifeboats

The loss of the *Arrow* highlighted once again the need for a motor lifeboat at Bridlington. For some years the fishing fleet had been growing. The sailing cobles had converted to engine power along with larger keelboats, which were also built with a deck. They fished further away from Bridlington in deeper water. The AGM of the Bridlington branch of the RNLI in 1926 witnessed an appeal by Coxswain Ernest Welburn to the RNLI for a motor lifeboat at Bridlington. He explained that the lifeboat and crew were at present greatly handicapped: a large fleet of motor fishing boats and their crews had to be looked after by the sailing lifeboat.

The RNLI in 1904 converted a rowing lifeboat into motor by fitting a 12 b.h.p. Fay and Bowen two-stroke engine. She carried out trials at Cowes, Isle of Wight which were described as very successful. Other trials took place which encouraged the RNLI to continue adapting lifeboats. The first purpose-built motor lifeboat went on service in 1909 but the development and installation of engines was restricted to the larger class of slipway, launched or afloat lifeboats. It wasn't until 1921 that a smaller 35-foot, self-righting, carriage-launched lifeboat was built, fitted with a Miller petrol motor. She was stationed at Eastbourne and proved to be very satisfactory. The crew in the motorised lifeboat were able to cover distances and speeds unattainable by the sailing and rowing lifeboats.

In 1929 Coxswain Welburn and his deputy Tom Hutchinson travelled to Ryde, where trials on a new lifeboat were taking place. Early in 1931 the RNLI sent word to the Bridlington station that a new motor lifeboat was to be delivered in June.

The Lifeboat *Stanhope Smart*

On 8 June 1931 the weather was fine and warm with a calm sea. Hundreds of people congregated to welcome the new lifeboat, *Stanhope Smart*. The T.S.S. *Yorkshire Man* and SS *Kernooza* led the welcome from the local boats, all blowing sirens. The crowds cheered and signal rockets were fired from the South Pier. The *George and Jane Walker* was launched to greet her replacement, sailing smartly across the harbour mouth, the scene of so much of her valiant work. The *George and Jane Walker* was the last sailing and rowing lifeboat to be stationed at Bridlington. She had served as the lifeboat for 32 years saving 60 lives. On Wednesday, 5 August 1931 the boat was sold at auction by Messrs Cranswick and Cranswick for £52 10s. 0d. to Mr S. Harrington of Leigh on Sea, who intended it to be converted into a houseboat for use on the River Thames.

20. Stanhope Smart *entering the harbour with the seas breaking across the canch and lifeboat, 11 January 1934.*

The *Stanhope Smart* lifeboat was named by Her Royal Highness Princess Mary, Countess of Harewood, on 5 August 1931 in front of a crowd of thousands. The ceremony took place near the Spa Royal Hall with a large party of dignitaries present. The proceedings were opened by Major Strickland, the President of Bridlington RNLI, followed by Cdr Drury OBE, Inspector of Lifeboats. As he began to speak the rain began to fall; because of the poor weather forecast, three very large umbrellas had been fixed over the platform. The Hon. George Colville, deputy chairman of the RNLI, then formally presented the lifeboat to the Bridlington lifeboat station and Mrs H. Harker, Mayoress of Bridlington, and the President of the Ladies Lifeboat Guild accepted her. After the dedication by Rev. Canon Topham, Her Royal Highness stepped forward into the heavy rain to name the *Stanhope Smart* and wished her 'God speed in her beneficent task', before releasing a bottle of champagne, which crashed over the lifeboat bow. Alderman H. Harker, Mayor of Bridlington, accorded a vote of thanks to Princess Mary. Sir George Shee seconded this, and the national anthem ended the formal ceremony. Princess Mary then left for Scarborough to conduct a similar naming ceremony on their new motorised lifeboat.

In the early afternoon the lifeboat tractor pulled the *Stanhope Smart* through the town to Trinity Cut, for her first practice launch as Bridlington's new lifeboat. After being put through her paces by the coxswain and crew, she beached on the south side, re carriaged and was taken to the boathouse on South Marine Drive. Coxswain and crew were full of praise, describing her performance during the practice as Splendid'.

The *Stanhope Smart* was 35 feet 6 inches long, 8 feet 10 inches beam; she had an English oak keel, mahogany planking, and ribs of Canadian rock elm. The planking was set diagonally forming two skins/hulls one inside the other; the outside hull of the boat was protected by a rubbing strake of rock elm. Between the two sets of planking were 100 watertight buoyancy tanks; the boat was divided into four watertight compartments, and fitted on deck were 15 steel buoyancy tanks, so the lifeboat was able to float even if half the keel was knocked out. The air boxes at her bow and stern gave buoyancy, as was the case with the old rowing and sailing lifeboats; if she capsized this buoyancy enabled the boat to right herself. She weighed 6.1 tons, fitted with a 35 b.h.p. Wayburn petrol engine giving a speed of 7.5 knots at full speed and a range of 100 miles. The crew of eight consisted of coxswain, second coxswain, first and second motor mechanics, bowman, signal man and two boatmen. She was able to carry her crew plus 30 survivors in bad weather.

By this time, the launch of the Bridlington lifeboat had become structured and an impressive operation. Gone were the days of frustration, waiting for horses or sufficient manpower to pull the lifeboat to the site of the wreck or down to the water's edge, knowing that the delay may result in the crew of the wreck perishing. The crew had been spontaneous volunteers; men fighting each other to gain a place on the lifeboat crew had now disappeared. When the coxswain was alerted to the need for the lifeboat he ran to the lifeboat house to fire the two signal rockets (maroons) calling the crew to the boathouse. In a very short space of time, day or night, the crew appeared from all directions, quickly and efficiently. The large wooden doors of the boathouse swung open, accompanied by the roar of the tractor being started. The lifeboat was taken to the beach, onboard her crew putting on their yellow oilskin coats and fastening the straps of their kapok lifejackets before checking that the ropes and gear were all in place for the task ahead.

The *Stanhope Smart* continued to work looking after the fishing fleet. Her first service call was on 3 November 1931 to escort the fishing keelboats *Felicity* and *Victory* into harbour through the heavy seas at the harbour entrance caused by the strong southerly gales. The extra weight of the *Stanhope Smart* caused the tractor difficulties in pulling the lifeboat and carriage up the slight incline at the Brunswick end of Bridge Street. But with ropes attached to the carriage and the help of the people watching, she was quickly pulled up the slope into Queen Street proceeding to Trinity Cut to launch. Once afloat with Coxswain Welburn in command, the new lifeboat rode the mountainous seas well. Her speed across the waves was commented on with pride.

Escorting the fishing cobles into harbour, when the wind was blowing gale force from the east or south-east, became a regular call for the *Stanhope Smart*. During one such call on 11 January 1934 crew man Frank Broadbent was washed out of the lifeboat by a huge breaking sea when escorting four fishing boats, *Protect Me II*, *Excelsior*, *Meggies* and *Victory* into harbour. The same wave almost capsized the lifeboat. Frank held onto one of the lifelines on the outside of the lifeboat's hull before being dragged back onboard by the other crew-members.

In September 1939 Ernest 'Brannie' Welburn retired, and Tom Hutchinson was voted to take over as coxswain by the traditional crew vote.

In the same month the declaration of war increased the dangers for the *Stanhope Smart* and her crew.

The Second World War

As with the First World War, all coastal navigation lights were turned off. Minefields were laid along the coast by ships of the Royal Navy. The Germans scattered mines wherever they could from aeroplanes or submarines, in order to attack the allied shipping along the coast.

The beaches were closed to the public, due to the threat of invasion by German troops on the low Holderness coastline. Notices stated:

No person shall for the purpose of recreation or pleasure, or as a casual wayfarer enter on any beach or foreshore, or enter upon any immediate approach to any such beach or foreshore.

The ban was in place because of underwater defences in the sea; in addition, the beaches were mined and covered with barbed wire barriers. Both the North and South Piers were also mined. At the harbour entrance a barge was moored each night. If the invasion came, the barge was to be sunk, thereby creating a barrier preventing any enemy boat from entering the harbour.

The fishing boats were able to sail without permission from the naval officer in charge of the district but the lifeboat had to ask! The new dangers in this war came from enemy aircraft and 'E' boats.

During the 1930s the lifeboat had averaged four service launches per year. In the first year of the war she was called out 14 times, mainly during the winter months when dark nights combined with bad weather. The winter of 1939/40 was one of the worst for over 20 years. Often the lifeboat crew were covered in freezing spray, which turned to ice on their oilskins and lifejackets, and they spent many hours searching without any means of making hot drinks or even protecting themselves from the elements.

One of the early lifeboat service calls came on 19 December 1939, at 7 p.m. Flares were observed approximately seven miles east-south-east of the harbour, to which the lifeboat was launched. After searching the area extensively the lifeboat returned to station. The message from the coastguards was that aeroplanes of the RAF had been carrying out night exercises. The Honorary Secretary of the lifeboat station Mr Charles Gray was reported as saying: 'we know there is a war on but such information could be passed to us then treated as confidential, all the lifeboats on the coast might have been launched without any need.'

On 11 January 1940 at 4.30 p.m. a message was picked up by radio that the S.S. *Pitwines* was being attacked off the coast by German aircraft firing at her with machine guns. She was asking for help and the crew were taking to the ship's boats. The lifeboat was launched at 5.20 p.m. after first seeking permission from the Royal Naval officer in charge of the district. The *Pitwines* reported her position as 17 miles south of Flamborough Head. After searching the area for several hours in pitch darkness, without any sign of the boat, the lifeboat returned to station.

The delay in launching the lifeboat was very frustrating. First, the message came that the lifeboat was needed, then permission to launch had to be obtained from the Royal Navy. The firing of maroons to summon the lifeboat crews was forbidden. Each man of the crew, together with helpers, had to be individually called, all adding to the time delay.

Despite all these problems the lifeboat crew were always ready. The very next day, 12 January 1940, the lifeboat was at sea again. A small convoy sailing along the coast had been attacked by enemy aircraft four miles east-north-east of Flamborough Head. Four vessels had been damaged, one a 10,000-ton steamer by a bomb dropped into the hold which had failed to explode. The crews had abandoned ship, taking to small boats. When the German aircraft left the area the crews were able to return to their ships and proceeded to London, and the lifeboat returned safely to station without being needed.

Two weeks later, on 29 January 1940 at 1.50 p.m. the lifeboat was requested to go to the aid of a vessel 12 miles south-east from Bridlington in a strong gale blowing from the east-south-east with heavy snow. The lifeboat proceeded to the position given, under the command of Coxswain Tom Hutchinson. They came alongside a steamer flying distress signals. She was the S.S. *Gripfast*. She had been attacked by enemy aircraft. Bullet holes and bomb damage were everywhere and steam could be seen escaping from broken pipes. They asked for a doctor as they had injured men on board. After putting two men on board to pilot her into Bridlington, they were told that the S.S. *Stainburn* had been sunk by enemy bombing, and that four men were adrift on a raft 10 miles south of his position. The lifeboat steamed through heavy seas and snow squalls, withstanding the atrocious conditions. The crew searched the area during which time a plane flew so low that the identification of the German aircraft was clearly seen, but the lifeboat was not fired on and the plane disappeared into the distance out to sea. After a long search for several hours in very poor weather, the lifeboat, finding nothing, returned into the Bay. The S.S. *Gripfast* asked the lifeboat to stand by her, while she attempted to enter harbour in the poor weather conditions. This was agreed, but the vessel missed the harbour entrance, striking the end of the South Pier, and was driven ashore, being stranded on the beach to the south of the harbour. The lifeboat returned to the beach with great difficulty in the severe weather and later coxswain Hutchinson described the 11 hours' service in atrocious weather as 'a very hazardous service'.

The lifeboat and lifeboat house had lucky escapes on more than one occasion.

On 23 August 1940, eight bombs were dropped by an enemy plane. They landed in a line from the beach, just in front of the Spa Royal Hall, across the harbour to Cliff Street. The pleasure boat *Royal Sovereign*, which had been moored alongside the South Pier, took a direct hit which blew her to pieces. A second bomb landed in a coble without detonating the fuse, and was removed by a naval officer stationed in Bridlington. Other damage was sustained by the *Britannia Hotel* and the *Cock and Lion* public house in Prince Street.

On 10 April 1941, 12 bombs dropped on the Hamilton and New Burlington Road area.

A stick of 14 bombs dropped in a line from the lower lifeboat slipway to the harbour mouth on 12 May 1941.

On 26 January 1941 the lifeboat was called out after distress flares had been seen off Hornsea. After a long search without success the lifeboat returned to Bridlington Harbour only to be informed that the vessel they had been searching for had been a French lifeboat under the orders of the Royal Navy. It had drifted onto the beach one mile north of Hornsea. The crew admitted that when the *Stanhope Smart* was close to them in the dark they were afraid to call out or show a light, as they thought the lifeboat was a German sea plane or 'E' boat from the sound made by her engine.

The lifeboat remained in harbour until daylight the following day, not wanting to go back to the beach in the dark on account of the obstructions and mines along the beach.

On 19 May 1941 it was reported that, for the lifeboat to be allowed to launch, a barbed wire barrier had to be removed from the foreshores and beach.

In November 1942, as the lifeboat was going down the slope to the South Beach, it fouled military telephone wires by pulling the top off an electrical standard and breaking the wires: 'O the joys of being a lifeboat man'.

As the War continued, so did the calls for the lifeboat. Vessels were machine-gunned by aircraft. Sightings of vessels in distress or reports of explosions at sea caused long arduous searches in bad weather. When the RAF air sea rescue launches based in Bridlington harbour were unable to leave harbour to go to the assistance of aircraft shot down into the sea, the lifeboat took their place.

With the ending of the Second World War the dangers that had been man-made came to an end but the War with the old enemy, the sea, continued.

During the summer of 1999 a gentleman visited the boathouse. After I had been talking to him for some time about the lifeboat station and the modern Mersey class lifeboat, I learnt that he had been on board the landing craft which had been in difficulty off Bridlington during the war. As we looked at the service boards in the lifeboat station, he quickly pointed to the entry for 3 December 1943, giving landing craft and nine lives rescued from shipwreck, of whom he had been one. After 56 years he had returned to say 'thank you'. Before leaving he put a donation in the lifeboat box, thereby helping to continue the work of saving life at sea.

The *Stanhope Smart* lifeboat ended her time at Bridlington in October 1947 after serving for 16 years. She was transferred to Padstow where she served as the station's No 2 lifeboat. She was not called on to make any rescue or service launches, and was sold out of the RNLI service in October 1951.

The *Tillie Morrison, Sheffield*

The new lifeboat was another first for the station. She was the first twin-engine, self-righting lifeboat to be stationed at Bridlington and also the first lifeboat to be named by Her Royal Highness Princess Marina, Duchess of Kent on 8 May 1948. The Lord Lieutenant of the East Riding, Lord Middleton, presided. Cdr P.E. Vaux, Chief Inspector of Lifeboats, described the boat, and then in the traditional way the boat was handed over to the RNLI by Mr James Morrison, nephew of the donors. She was formally received by Sir Godfrey Baring, chairman of the RNLI, and then received on behalf of the Bridlington lifeboat station by Mr J.M. Deheer, Chairman of the Bridlington branch. The service of dedication was led by the Most Rev. C. F. Garbett, Archbishop of York. In naming the boat, the Duchess of Kent said, 'When hearing that Bridlington was to have a new lifeboat, I made a point of being here for the ceremony. Though I have visited several lifeboat stations throughout the country, this is the first time I have been asked to name a lifeboat and I am particularly pleased that we should be at Bridlington in the East Riding of Yorkshire. I now have great pleasure in naming this lifeboat 'Tillie Morrison, Sheffield'. I wish her and her crew God-speed in their work of rescue.' Bringing the ceremony to a close, a vote of thanks to the Duchess was proposed by Councillor F.F. Milner, Mayor of Bridlington, and seconded by Col A. D. Burnett Brown, secretary of the RNLI.

The *Tillie Morrison, Sheffield* was built in Cowes, Isle of Wight, at the yard of J.S. White, and cost £10,573. The donation to the RNLI by Mr James and Mr David Morrison of Sheffield, in memory of their sister, was used to fund the lifeboat.

21. Tillie Morrison, Sheffield *with crew and helpers. Left to right: S. Dodgson, W. Hutchinson, R. Simpson, G. Adamson, W. Newby, R. Redhead, J. Robinson, T. Hutchinson, H. Hutchinson, D. Smith and F. Johnson.*

The design of this Liverpool class of lifeboat derived from the development from the old single engine carriage lifeboat.

She was 35 feet 6 inches long, 10 feet beam, and weighed 7.25 tons. The materials used to build her were very similar to those used for *Stanhope Smart*. The hull of the *Tillie Morrison, Sheffield* was divided into eight watertight compartments and carried 156 air cases to provide buoyancy in case of damage to the hull. She would self-right herself, if capsized, in four seconds. She had a small shelter extending aft from the engine room canopy, which provided some protection for two or three of the crew. A half-ton water ballast tank was built into the hull, allowing the boat to launch on an even keel. The tank filled with seawater as the boat launched, which helped her to trim stern lower in the water, enabling the boat to handle better at sea. She was fitted with twin 18 b.h.p. Wayburn petrol engines, each one driving an 18-inch diameter by 16.5 pitch propeller, which turned in tunnels built into the hull to protect the propellers when in shallow water. The boat had a speed of 7.34 knots with a range of 70 miles. This was the first lifeboat for about 100 years that did not carry a full set of sails as a secondary means of propulsion. She was able to carry 30 survivors together with her crew of eight. An innovation was the wireless or radio-telephone, which enabled the lifeboat crew to be in constant contact with the shore.

Lifeboats can be called upon in all weather conditions, as was the case on 27 November 1948. Through combined help, the post master at Barmston rang the harbour master at Bridlington informing him that the fishing vessel *Raith Castle* was ashore one mile north of Barmston in thick fog. Visibility was down to fifty yards, wind southerly force one or less, sea slight. At 11.40 a.m. the lifeboat was launched with Coxswain Tom Hutchinson in command. One hour later, at 12.40 p.m., the lifeboat reported via 'wireless' that she was escorting the steam drifter *Raith Castle* BF 486, with a crew of ten on board, back to Bridlington harbour. At 1.05 p.m. both boats entered harbour safely. This was the first time on record that the Bridlington lifeboat had used radio/wireless in connection with a service launch.

The *Tillie Morrison, Sheffield* was stationed here for five years, launching on service 23 times, mainly to the local fishing fleet. The service launch on 19 August 1952 was to be her last at Bridlington. The Flamborough lifeboat station and its lifeboat were out of service because the slipway was being modified and lengthened to accept a new lifeboat. At 5.08 p.m., the coastguards requested the Bridlington lifeboat to launch and go to the aid of two teenage girl bathers, both ironically from Sheffield, who were being swept out to sea from Thornwick Bay on the Flamborough Headland. There was a north-north-easterly gale blowing, which had caused an extremely rough sea. On reaching North Landing the lifeboat met an RAF air sea rescue launch making her way to Bridlington with the body of one of the girls onboard. A semaphore message from the coastguards, on the cliff, asked the lifeboat to search the area. The lifeboat proceeded westwards from North Landing to Thornwick Bay and onto Little Thornwick Bay, finding nothing. Coxswain Newby continued the search to the east. On entering Thornwick Bay, the *Tillie Morrison, Sheffield* was hit by a huge wave; the deep swell and vicious sea had been caused by the ebbing tide together with the strong wind and the backwash from the cliffs. On seeing the wave approaching the lifeboat, the coxswain shouted, 'Hang on, water coming'. The wave, described by an eyewitness as being like a mountain, struck the lifeboat broadside on, capsizing her. Of the crew of seven, five were thrown into the sea. On hearing the warning shout from the coxswain, second mechanic Derek Nightingale wedged himself under the engine room canopy. The coxswain managed to hold onto the steering wheel as the boat capsized, but the force with which she righted herself threw him overboard. While gathering himself, mechanic Nightingale heard shouts and found one of the crew, Herbert Smith, hanging onto the lifeboat guardrail. As he got him halfway into the boat Nightingale saw coxswain and the bowman Robert Redhead struggling in the water but the swell carried them away before he could reach them. Returning to Smith he managed to pull him on board. When the lifeboat capsized, the engines had cut out; the lifeboat's anchor fell out of the lifeboat into the sea, unintentionally anchoring the boat. Smith, though injured, took the wheel while mechanic Nightingale started the engines, cut the anchor cable and pulled all the loose ropes on board. They then sailed clear of the broken water. They could see that some of the crew had already made it to shore, no one else could be seen in the water, so they set off for Bridlington. Before they had travelled far they that found the boat was taking in water, so they headed back to Thornwick Bay. During the short passage one of the engines stopped. The drogue was streamed to allow the swell to carry the lifeboat onto the beach, where a crowd of willing helpers, supervised by Coxswain Cowling of the Flamborough lifeboat, hauled her up.

The five lifeboat men who had been thrown out, all managed to reach the shore. Bowman Robert P. Redhead had been injured and died shortly afterwards. Coxswain Newby was kept in hospital overnight. The two girl swimmers, for whom the lifeboat had launched, both drowned.

Lifeboat men carried Robert Redhead to his final resting place in Bridlington Cemetery following the service at the Central Methodist Church in Chapel Street. The service was attended by crewmen from six Yorkshire lifeboat stations, together with representatives from the RNLI and many other local organisations connected with the sea. His headstone is a marble lifeboat man which stands as testimony to his bravery and self-sacrifice.

A brass plaque was placed in the lifeboat house and unveiled by Lady Hotham, wife of the president of the Bridlington RNLI. It is inscribed 'In memory of Robert P. Redhead, Bowman of the *Tillie Morrison, Sheffield* who lost his life whilst on service August 19th 1952'.

After the tragic accident, temporary repairs were made to the lifeboat's damaged starboard side. Later she sailed to Whitby for permanent repairs. She was escorted by the fishing keelboat *Melba*. After the repairs were completed she was transferred to Llandudno, where she served until 1959, being launched 17 times on service saving eight lives, before being sold out of RNLI service in September 1959.

The *Tillie Morrison, Sheffield II*

On 22 August 1952 a lifeboat from the RNLI reserve fleet, *Annie, Ronald and Isabella Forrest*, entered Bridlington Harbour under the command of Coxswain Walter Newby. She was 17 years old, 35 feet 6 inches long by 10 feet 3 inches beam, single engine Liverpool class lifeboat. She had served at St Abb's lifeboat station for 13 years, before joining the reserve fleet. She was not a self-righting lifeboat. After some time getting used to the lifeboat, the Bridlington crew decided she performed very well. They asked the RNLI for the new Bridlington lifeboat to be of the same type and design.

22. *The* Tillie Morrison, Sheffield II *flag day exercises, 1966.*

23. *The* Tillie Morrison, Sheffield II. *The man at the left of the photo is Brian Bevan, later to become Superintendent Coxswain of Humber Lifeboat Station, the only man ever to be awarded the RNLI's Gold, Silver and Bronze medals in the same year, 1966. Note the Souwester hat and kapok lifejackets.*

In accordance with their wishes the new Bridlington lifeboat was a Liverpool type, non-self-righting, twin-engine lifeboat which was built by Groves and Gutteridges in Cowes, Isle of Wight. This class of lifeboat had been first introduced in 1945 and after extensive use by lifeboat crews in hazardous weather conditions around the coast they soon became more popular with lifeboat crews than the similar self-righting type.

The Bridlington Honorary Secretary, Mr J.M. Deheer (whose son, John, is a branch committee member today), was informed of the decision to name the new lifeboat at Cowes, where she had been built. The reason was that the Crane Wharf jetty, alongside the North Pier where her predecessor was named, had been declared unsafe by the Ministry of Transport.

Bridlington was well represented at the naming ceremony on 12 May 1953. The branch Chairman, Honorary Secretary, members of the Ladies Lifeboat Guild and others were present. Sir Godfrey Baring, chairman of the RNLI committee of management, presided. After Cdr E. W. Middleton, district inspector of lifeboats, had described the lifeboat, the vicar of Holy Trinity Church, Cowes, the Rev. C.E Paterson blessed her, and she was named *Tillie Morrison, Sheffield II* by Mrs W. D. Gale, honorary secretary of the Cowes Ladies Lifeboat Guild.

The new lifeboat cost £14,481, paid from the legacy of Mr A. Whitaker of Bradford, and funds of the RNLI.

There had been a suggestion that the new lifeboat should be named *Robert Redhead*. The original *Tillie Morrison, Sheffield* had been presented by two brothers in memory of their late sister and, when the second brother died, he left £5,000 for the upkeep of the lifeboat bearing his sister's name on the east coast of Yorkshire. The legal obligations had to be honoured, so the name *Tillie Morrison, Sheffield II* was chosen by the RNLI.

The new lifeboat was 35 feet 6 inches long. She was powered by twin 20 b.h.p. Ferry diesel engines, her beam was 10 feet 8 inches, and her end boxes were much lower than her predecessor, as she was not intended to self-right. Tests on the new lifeboat had shown no loss of stability until inclined at an angle in excess of 90 degrees. The hull was divided into six watertight compartments. Around the watertight deck were fitted 152 air cases, to ensure that she would remain buoyant even in the event of serious damage to the hull. When the seas broke over her she would quickly free herself of water by means of 20 scuppers fitted to each side of the boat at deck level. She weighed in service conditions 8.3 tonnes and had a maximum speed of 7.5 knots, carrying enough fuel to give the boat the ability to cover 120 nautical miles. She had a crew of seven, and in bad weather could take on 45 survivors; in good weather this could be increased to 55 survivors.

The *Tillie Morrison, Sheffield II* arrived at Bridlington on 17 June 1953; the *Annie Ronald and Isabella Forrest* was launched and put in the harbour. The new lifeboat took her place on the carriage, after slight adjustments were made. The lifeboat was exercised for the first time under the command of Coxswain Newby.

Within only one month she had begun her work of saving lives. On 13 July a message was received from the harbour staff that a small boat was requiring assistance off Skipsea. The coastguards were contacted but had no knowledge of any missing vessel. The weather was overcast with mist and heavy rain, and the decision was taken to launch the lifeboat to investigate, at 8.25 a.m. The lifeboat launched to search the area. At 11.15 a.m. a signal was received from the lifeboat, 'returning to Bridlington with small boat the *Firefly* in tow and having 4 survivors on board'.

The tasks of the lifeboat were, and still are, ever changing. Leisure boats were also from time to time in need of help.

On 7 August 1955, the Honorary Secretary was informed, at 12 noon, that the yacht *Regina* had left the harbour and not returned on the ebbing tide. He immediately alerted the coxswain after which he telephoned the coastguard. The coastguard reported that they had seen the yacht drifting southwards towards the Smithic Sands. At the time there were several light steamers anchored, sheltering from the weather in the Bay. The wind was north-westerly, force 7 to gale force 8. The maroons were fired to call the crew, and the boat was afloat and proceeding at 12.30 p.m. in the direction given by the coastguard. Nearing the coaster *Daniel M* they were given the position of the yacht by this vessel. The yacht had miraculously driven across the Smithic Sands and was still afloat, but obviously nearly full of water. Owing to the shortage of time the coxswain decided that the only way to get to the boat before she sank

24. *The author with lifelong friend Brian Bevan showing the changing style of oilskins, now with hooded top and trousers and new 'life belt' in 1967.*

was to proceed himself over the Smithic Sands. This was cleverly done and the two crew were taken off the yacht, onto the lifeboat. The yacht was then taken in tow and the lifeboat proceeded southwards to come round the south end of the Smithic Sands. But on the way the yacht, despite efforts to save her, foundered. The lifeboat proceeded to the harbour to land the two survivors before returning to the South Beach to re-carriage and return to station.

The coxswain remarked that this was the second time within six weeks that this yacht had been in trouble owing to the crew's lack of sea knowledge.

The ever-changing challenge for the lifeboat continued during the late 1950s and into the following years. The need to evacuate injured fishermen and seamen from vessels passing up and down the coast increased. Given the shelter of Flamborough Head, the Bay was a natural area to transfer injured or sick people from one boat to another.

On Saturday, 9 April 1966, the maroons were fired at about 7.30 p.m. I ran to the boathouse just in time to help connect the tractor to the lifeboat carriage. As the boat was pulled out of the lifeboat house, I ran upstairs to the crew room to put on my oilskins and thigh boots. Then without thinking ran down onto the South Beach, from where the lifeboat is normally launched, only to find myself all alone – no boat, no crew, no people watching. I suddenly realised that they were spring tides and the sea was crashing right up to the sea wall, leaving no beach from which to launch the lifeboat. On occasions like this plan 'B' came into action; the lifeboat was taken to the harbour and launched from Gummers Wharf. Being upstairs at the boathouse

I had missed the fact that the boat had turned left out of the boathouse towards the harbour and not right, as normal, onto the South Beach. Changing direction I ran in oilskins and thigh boots along the seafront to the harbour to be in time to help with manoeuvring the carriage and lifeboat around the end of the RAF shed (now Rag's Restaurant) before taking my place in the boat to launch down the slipway into the harbour.

The call had been received, by a radio message to the coastguard, asking to transfer an injured fisherman from the North Sea trawler *Ross Cormorant* to hospital. We met up with the trawler one-mile east of the harbour; transferring the man onto the lifeboat, we then entered the harbour and passed the injured seaman onto a waiting ambulance.

This was the last time the lifeboat was ever launched into the harbour for a service call. Today, because of the difficulties of manoeuvring the lifeboat and carriage down into the harbour, plan 'B', the alternative emergency launch site, is down the Belvedere boat compound slipway, Belvedere Parade, at the south end of the foreshores.

With the increase in Medi vacs (medical evacuations), some of us had attended first-aid classes and were qualified to administer first-aid at sea, which brings to mind the following service call for *Tillie Morrison, Sheffield II*.

I will not name the boat, but suffice to say it was a deep-sea trawler on passage from Hull to the Icelandic fishing grounds. The coastguards requested the lifeboat to launch to transfer a casualty ashore, the maroons were duly fired, and the lifeboat under the command of Coxswain King was launched to rendezvous with the trawler in the Bay. The two first-aid qualified crew-members to board the trawler were Dennis Atkins and myself (Dennis known affectionately to everybody as 'Twiggy' because of his slightly rotund figure); by trade he was a painter. Going alongside the trawler, Dennis and I went on board with a Neil Robertson stretcher and a first-aid kit. We were taken into the cabin where we found the injured crewman, laid out drunk, with a suspected broken leg. He was shouting, swearing and not allowing anyone to touch him, including Dennis and myself. We still had on our oilskins and lifejackets and the small cabin was very hot so we took off our oilskin coats, whilst deciding how to overcome this difficult problem. At this point the injured crewman stopped shouting obscenities, calmed down and allowed us to examine him. We suddenly realised that Dennis was wearing his painter's clean white jacket and trousers and the patient thought he was a doctor! Quickly we examined the casualty, confirming he had a broken leg. We gave him an injection of morphine, which in those days we carried on the lifeboat for the relief of pain. Then without losing any time but with some difficulty, we got him onto the Neil Robertson stretcher. He had calmed down dramatically which was very convenient, as the only way to get him out of the cabin and onto the deck was to physically lift him, with the help of the trawler crew, vertically round two sharp right-angle corners. Then along the companionway and out onto the deck of the trawler, we manhandled him over the fishing gear across the ship's rail and onto the deck of the lifeboat, before returning to harbour and transferring him to a waiting ambulance on the South Pier.

Without the white painter's overall that Dennis was wearing that day, the job could have been very difficult in the small confined cabin space, with a drunk, uncooperative patient.

After each launch, the lifeboat was taken back to the boathouse, where the tractor winched the carriage and boat back into it. During this operation the lifeboat on its carriage was normally steered by the head launcher, using a pole attached to the opposite end of the lifeboat carriage. When the boat was safely in the boathouse, the crew hanged their oilskins on an old-fashioned drying frame on which the kapok lifejackets were also put. This frame was hoisted up into the roof space for the oilskins and lifejackets to dry out. Very often, the next time they were needed they were as wet, cold and damp as they had previously been when they had been taken off. This improved dramatically when the heated extension to the boathouse was built in 1979.

The construction of the *Tillie Morrison, Sheffield II* was of watertight sections. Each one had a brass screw on the outside of the hull. After each launch these were all checked in turn, to make sure each compartment was free water and that the hull hadn't been damaged. The boat was washed in soapy fresh water to get rid of any salt water that was on the boat. All ropes and gear were checked for any damage. The *Tillie Morrison, Sheffield II* had lots of brass work, cleats, compass, etc and each week the crew would take great pride in keeping all the brass work clean which shone against the varnished top side of the boat. It was not unusual during this work to hear a shout from outside and then to see a tray of pint glasses full of beer being passed across the hedge from the Yacht Club next door by the steward Jack Allan.

She was a very good sea boat, well loved by all who sailed in her, and the first Bridlington lifeboat to make over 100 service launches. She served at Bridlington for 14 years. As technology moves on so must the lifeboats. In July 1967 it was announced that one of the modern 37-foot Oakley self-righting lifeboats was to be transferred to the Bridlington Station. On 3 September 1967 *Tillie Morrison, Sheffield II* sailed from Bridlington for the last time, bound for the RNLI reserve fleet.

In 1969 she was purchased by the Sumner, New Zealand Lifeboat Institution and was transported 12,000 miles on the deck of the cargo vessel *Gladstone Star* to start her new career as a lifeboat on the other side of the world.

On arrival at Littleton, New Zealand, she was transferred to C.W.F. Hamilton's boatyard for modifications to the hull, engines and gearbox. Radar and radio communications were fitted. With this work completed, on 21 January 1970 she was ready for service as a lifeboat. Later that year, 28 November, she was renamed at a ceremony presided over by Mr. N.E. Kirk, Esq, MP, who later became Prime Minister of New Zealand. After a number of speeches, Mr Kirk introduced Mr C.I. Denham, aged 90 years, the oldest member of the Sumner Lifeboat Institution. With the assistance of Coxswain J. Kerr they renamed the lifeboat *Rescue III* which was followed by a dedication service, led by the Roman Catholic Vicar General of Christchurch. Following the service, the lifeboat was blessed by the Bishop of Christchurch.

Rescue III served as a lifeboat in Sumner, New Zealand until 1992, when she was replaced by another lifeboat from the UK. She was sold out of service to Mr David Chadfield of New Plymouth, Taranaki. Today she is used to take passengers around a seal island just off the coast, as well as for general cruises to celebrate weddings, anniversaries etc.

My wife Carol and I, while on holiday in New Zealand in February 2000, were fortunate enough to visit Sumner lifeboat station, which was established in 1898, and we met the crew and helpers together with Walter J. Baguley the Hon. Secretary of Sumner lifeboat station. We had first met when he visited Bridlington lifeboat station on 14 July 1989. Carol and I then went on to pay a very nostalgic visit to New Plymouth, to the boat I still remember with affection, *Tillie Morrison, Sheffield II*, the first lifeboat I was fortunate enough to serve on, as a young crew-member. David Chadfield is very proud of the history behind his boat, informing visitors to Taranaki from around the world of its proud history at Bridlington, East Yorkshire, England. David is keeping her in shipshape condition, which is a credit to him and the builders of this 52-year-old boat.

David's grandson has the job of cleaning the brass work, which still gleams as it used to when the crew in Bridlington cleaned it.

The *William Henry and Mary King*

Arthur Dick, the Honorary Secretary of the Bridlington lifeboat station, was informed on 17 August 1967 that, after refits at Fletcher's yard Lowestoft, the lifeboat, *William Henry and Mary King* (official number O.N.980) would sail for Bridlington on 1 September 1967 to take over as Bridlington lifeboat.

The *William Henry and Mary King* had started service life as Cromer, Norfolk No 2 lifeboat. She had been built by J. S. White, of Cowes, Isle of Wight in 1964 to the revolutionary design of Richard Oakley, the RNLI's naval architect, at a cost of £33,000, paid for from a legacy of the late Mr J. G. King, of Sutton, Surrey, together with funds from the RNLI.

Before the new Oakley design, the choice of lifeboat had been between the non self-righting design, which had high inherent stability and was unlikely to capsize, but, if capsized, would not self-right. The second choice was the self-righting boat, which of necessity had less inherent stability and was therefore more likely to capsize, but if this occurred the boat would self-right. The Oakley design managed to combine both these qualities into one, producing a lifeboat which had greater initial stability than the non self-righting Liverpool type it was to replace and would recover from capsize by an ingenious system of shifting water ballast.

On launching, one and a half tons of water is shipped by the lifeboat and stored in a tank near the keel, where it combines with the weight of the engines to provide initial stability. Should the boat capsize, the water ballast is transferred through special valves to her righting tank in the port side of the lifeboat. If the capsize is to starboard then the transfer of water, when the boat is healed over to about 165 degrees, causes the boat to complete a 360-degree roll to come up-right. With a port capsize, the transfer commences at about 110 degrees to arrest the capsize and thus return the boat to an even keel.

The construction of the boat's hull was two thicknesses of African mahogany diagonally laid. She was 37 feet long, beam 11 feet 6 inches and weight 12.45 tons. Her two engines were four-cylinder, 52 b.h.p. Ford Porbeagle diesel motors, giving her a maximum speed of 8.16 knots and a range of 77.5 miles. She had a crew of seven men: first and second coxswain, first and second mechanic, three crewmen.

The *William Henry and Mary King* was named at Cromer, on 8 July 1965 by Her Royal Highness Princess Marina, Duchess of Kent. Mr J.H. Rounce, chairman of the Branch, had opened the proceedings; Mr T.H. Sutton presented the lifeboat to the RNLI on behalf of the executors of the late donor. The lifeboat was accepted by Cdr H.F.B. Grenfell, a vice-president of the Institution, who in turn handed her into the care of the Cromer branch for use on the number 2 lifeboat station and Dr Vaughan received her on behalf of the Cromer lifeboat station. This was followed by the familiar RNLI service of dedication, led by the Rev. C.W.J. Searle-Barnes, vicar of Cromer, during which the Rt. Rev. W.L.S. Fleming, Bishop of Norwich, dedicated the lifeboat. Mr Rounce then invited Her Royal Highness to step forward and name the lifeboat *William Henry and Mary King*.

While on station at Cromer she made 12 service launches saving one life. In 1967 the RNLI decided to close the number 2 station and transfer the boat to Bridlington, where she duly arrived on the evening of 2 September 1967 after a stormy passage from Lowestoft against a northerly gale.

The day after she arrived, whilst on exercise undergoing sea trials and familiarising ourselves with the boat, we were called out on service to the assistance of a small boat being blown out to sea by a strong westerly wind off Ulrome. This was the first service of many to be carried out by the Bridlington lifeboat, the *William Henry and Mary King*.

It didn't take long for us to get used to the new boat. Coxswain John King expressed his delight with the extra speed and the good handling of the boat.

Offshore lifeboats have two numbers: an official number, introduced after the stringent self-righting tests were introduced in 1887, and an operational class number. O.N. 980 was her official number and 37-13 the operational number. For obvious reasons she did not display her operational number in large black figures on the side of the engine room canopy as all other lifeboats do (Unlucky 13).

The *William Henry and Mary King*, a conventionally built lifeboat, changed during the time she served as Bridlington lifeboat. In 1971 a small canvas cover was fitted aft from the top of the engine room canopy windscreen, to give some protection to the crew from the wind and weather. This was replaced in 1982 by a larger metal frame and canvas wheelhouse, which folded down to deck level, enabling the lifeboat to fit into the lifeboat house. This was made with the help of two Hull businessmen, Mr David Jordan who made the cover and Mr Alan Shaw whose firm made the framework. The most important addition to the equipment carried by the lifeboat was radar, which was fitted at the normal refit, but, because of the complex nature of fitting the radar, this refit work took longer than normal. She left Bridlington for Amble in March and returned on 22 November 1977.

Fitting radar into lifeboats had been a very difficult task for the RNLI. The problem was to find a radar set and ancillary equipment to fit into a relatively small lifeboat, in which space was limited and weight critical, with the low boat deck often awash with sea water. The radar set to solve the problem was the Decca 060. The rotating scanner was mounted on a folding tripod on top of the engine room canopy, which collapsed down when the boat went back into the boathouse. The cost of the radar was £1,250, the gift from the legacy of the late John Heron.

The *William Henry and Mary King* carried the most up-to-date radios to keep in constant contact with the coastguards and for use when working with helicopters, fixed wing aircraft, the Royal Navy, local boats and of course casualties.

25. *The* William Henry and Mary King *shortly after she arrived at Bridlington, September 1967.*

26. *The* William Henry and Mary King, *1979, fitted with radar etc.*

She was also fitted with a small water heater, which meant that the crew, on long service calls or during freezing cold conditions, for the first time were now able to have a hot drink. Crew-member Paul Staveley was very adept at making hot drinks when the boat was pitching violently in bad weather. Occasionally he did express his annoyance at spilling the hot contents of a mug over himself while doing so in such conditions.

The *William Henry and Mary King* became a well-liked boat. As the technology moved on the boat became a far more efficient tool for saving lives and giving help to others. The Medal/Vellum services during this period are testimonies of her capabilities.

October 1975 saw the retirement of Coxswain John King, on health grounds. I was asked by the crew to put myself forward as a candidate to fill the vacant position of coxswain. The traditional vote by crew-members and helpers of the station was held, at which the vote was unanimous. On 6 November 1975 I took over as coxswain of the Bridlington lifeboat. Dennis Atkins, who had served as the lifeboat crew-member for 13 years and had been the last bowman at Bridlington had been voted in to the position of second coxswain.

The fishing fleet of traditional Yorkshire cobles and trawlers was still the main work the lifeboat was tasked with.

On 1 December 1975 there had been a hard frost overnight when the fishing fleet sailed. With the dawn, a crimson red sky broke across the Bay. The light wind increased to gale force. At 11.15 a.m. the maroons were fired to call the lifeboat crew to the boathouse. There was an increasing heavy, breaking swell at the harbour entrance, while the wind was south-easterly in direction and storm force 10. Huge seas were crashing over the North Pier into the harbour.

The lifeboat escorted the open cobles into harbour using the drogue (a sea anchor). The coble *Joshann* lifted on the crest of a breaking wave and surfed at speed nearly into the harbour, fortunately keeping in a straight line had she broached; the outcome could have been far different. The lifeboat returned to escort the coble *Calarias*. As she entered harbour waves caught her and she was washed broadside on into the harbour. The next coble was the *Georgina*. She was knocked over by the breaking swell, laying her rail down and taking onboard some water when at the harbour mouth, but even with water onboard she still managed to enter harbour safely. The keelboats followed, taking a battering from the breaking south-easterly swell. One by one they reached the safety of the harbour. The lifeboat crew had been on escort duty to the local fishing fleet for six hours by the time she was rehoused and ready for service at 6.00 p.m.

The work of the RNLI has always been to help anyone in need, irrespective of nationality, religion or status. During the so-called Cold War, on 2 September 1976 at 4.30 p.m. the coastguards informed us by telephone that a Russian trawler, which had been fishing in the North Sea, had a sick man onboard and was making for Bridlington Bay, estimated time of arrival 9.00 p.m. After the first telephone call we managed to find a willing Russian interpreter from the local Lada car Importers Satra Motors, where some of the lifeboat crew worked and with whom we had very good relations. The crew were assembled at 8.00 p.m. and *William Henry and Mary King* was launched at 8.15 p.m., having onboard the interpreter. We made our way to a Russian trawler sheltering from the northerly gales in the Bay; she was one of a fleet

27. Lowering the Lifeboat down Levits Hill, which was covered with snow and ice.

of 30 that had been fishing off the East Yorkshire coast at that time. The interpreter was put onboard to pinpoint the whereabouts of the trawler with the sick man and to make radio contact; contact through the coastguards had been limited and vague, due to the language difficulty. The interpreter came back onboard the lifeboat and a course was set to the position given by the interpreter, which was two miles east of North Smithic Buoy. The weather outside the Bay, because of the northerly gale, was poor, there was a deep swell with northerly winds force 8, and as a result of the weather conditions both boats dodged back into the Bay. When in calmer water we went alongside the trawler to transfer the interpreter, after some time we managed, with difficulty, to get the sick man Oleg Lopatkin (43) onboard the lifeboat. We returned to Bridlington harbour where the Russian seaman, with a suspected kidney complaint, was handed into the care of the doctor and waiting ambulance. The lifeboat returned to station ready for service at 2.00 a.m.

On 3 January 1978, six cobles and three keelboats were at sea. The wind was westerly force 9, gusting 10. The Honorary Secretary Arthur Dick asked for the lifeboat to be launched, which it was at 7.15 a.m. The cobles had been working nets between Hornsea and Mappleton, and three of the cobles started to return to Bridlington under the lee of the low cliffs. The fourth coble *Sea Witch* had broken down with engine trouble. We went alongside in difficult conditions, managing to take off two young boys,* aged 13 and 15, to minimise any danger on the journey

---

* One of the boys was not put off by this ordeal. Paul Langley went on to become a Bridlington fisherman, now owning and running his own boat, catching shellfish.

back to the harbour. We also passed a towrope. Because of the wind and swell the speed of the tow back to Bridlington was reduced to about four knots. The lifeboat with the coble under tow entered the harbour safely at 1 p.m. At that time we were asked by the coastguards to escort a Dutch beam trawler into the Bay and to a safe anchorage, after which the skipper was transferred ashore, in the lifeboat, to arrange for engine repairs to be carried out.

On 10 October 1980, the lifeboat launched to a Belgium trawler with an injured fisherman onboard, caused by the fishing gear dropping on to his foot. The wind was north-easterly force 6 with a gale warning in operation. The trawler reported his position as 36 miles due east of Flamborough Head. The lifeboat rendez-voused with the boat 24 miles due east of Flamborough Head; the injured man was transferred with difficulty because of the weather conditions and the nature of his injury.

On 23 January 1984, the lifeboat was called out to escort the coble *Valhalla*. She had been reported by coastguards as making heavy weather off Skipsea. The wind was south-easterly force 8 with a heavy swell; the coble was escorted safely into harbour at 10.15 a.m. The weather deteriorated throughout the day. At 5.00 p.m. the lifeboat was once again asked to launch – the local keelboat *Margaret H* was making for Bridlington harbour. The lifeboat launched at 5.10 p.m.,* at which time Flamborough coastguards reported easterly winds of 45 knots gusting 50 knots. We met up with the *Margaret H* outside the Bay and then at reduced speed, because of the weather conditions, escorted her back into the Bay. The boat was being buffeted constantly by the large breaking easterly swell. Coastguards and the lifeboat illuminated the entrance for *Margaret H* with parachute flares. The lifeboat then returned to station, was refuelled and back ready for service at midnight.

On the weekend of 12 July 1987 the crew of the lifeboat were issued with personal radio paging devices, which would help to summon the crew faster and therefore speed up the launching of the lifeboat. The 'paging bleepers' are activated by a telephone call to a central number they were given by British Telecom. The cost of the system was funded by donations. A similar paging system is in use today, and as a back-up the two maroons that have been in use for over 150 years are still fired.

On 22 January 1988, coastguards requested the lifeboat launch for a medical evacuation from the Dutch minesweeper *Drachton* who was steaming towards Flamborough Head. We made arrangements to meet the minesweeper at the north end of the Bay, transferring the casualty plus one other seaman, a nurse. The lifeboat returned to Bridlington harbour, once again transferring the casualty into a waiting ambulance.

Only 18 days before this service to the minesweeper, the lifeboat was used in conjunction with the bomb disposal unit of the Royal Navy. The Scarborough-registered trawler *Silver Line*, whilst fishing 13 miles north-east of Flamborough Head on 4 January 1988, caught a seven-foot German mine in their nets. After lowering the net, containing the mine, gingerly back into the water, they towed their net at a safe distance behind their boat to a position three miles off Bridlington before lowering it, on the instructions of the coastguards, to the seabed, marking its position with a buoy. The Royal Navy bomb disposal team from Portsmouth had been contacted and arrived at Bridlington on the morning of 5 January 1988. The lifeboat was asked to

---

* Two launches to different incidents on the same day for the offshore lifeboat.

28. *The* William Henry and Mary King *with crew, 1980: Brian Cundall, Tony Ayre, Claud Sharp, Rod Stott, Dennis Atkins, the author and Paul Staveley.*

act as mother ship to their small inflatable boat. The lifeboat launched at midday and proceeded to the area three miles off Bridlington, where the Royal Navy diver swam down to investigate the mine. After doing so he attached a detonating charge with a delay fuse to the mine, which gave him time to swim to the surface and evacuate to a safe distance in the inflatable boat. When the mine exploded, the noise was heard all over Bridlington and surrounding area.

The mine had been a German 'D' mine, dropped by the Luftwaffe during the Second World War. These mines were primarily used against shipping as a seabed mine, or could be used as a conventional bomb. It was seven feet long 26-inch diameter packed with 670lbs of Hexonite high explosive. The casing was made of Rhinemetal, which was very strong and did not corrode. These mines were booby-trapped in many ways to prevent anyone disarming them. There were normally detonated by magnetic and acoustic systems. A ship passing over the area where the mine had been laid would detonate the mine.

During my 35 years' voluntary service on the lifeboat this was one of four such incidents involving wartime mines, one of which had washed ashore just to the west of South Landing, Flamborough in November 1992. Thankfully the Royal Navy bomb disposal teams detonated all the mines safely and without incident.

On 15 December 1988, the *William Henry and Mary King* was replaced; she had carried out 290 service calls in 22 years' service at Bridlington, saving 83 lives. She had been the busiest lifeboat Bridlington had ever had. Her predecessor *Tillie Morrison, Sheffield II* had held the record of 106 service launches.

The *William Henry and Mary King* was kept in a warehouse on Bessingby industrial estate until 1 February 1989 when she sailed for Seahouses to join the reserve fleet.

On 1 August (Yorkshire day) 1991, the *William Henry and Mary King* was lowered into position on the Drayton Park primary school playground, Islington, London. The school had raised £6,000 in order to transport the boat from Poole, in Dorset, and convert it into a play and educational area for the school children. She quickly became a local landmark, is used daily and much loved by the children.

The school is known as 'the school with the boat' and is much sought after as a result. Since it was developed as a play structure, the boat has become an integral part of playtimes for the children from the nursery upwards. The youngest children have a special playtime in the afternoons devoted to 'boat play'. The boat is regularly maintained and painted by volunteers. The lifeboat forms the school's logo and is on all stationery, jumpers etc. and whenever the school is in the news the children are photographed on or around the *William Henry and Mary King*.

6

The Move away from
Conventional Lifeboat Design

The lifeboat possesses special qualities, distinguishing it from all other boats. Chief among these are the self-righting and self-emptying principles. Stability, resulting from breadth of beam and the construction of the boat, will do much to render a boat safe in rough seas and tempestuous weather. When a boat has to face mighty rollers which turn it up until it stands straight on end, like a rearing horse, or even tumble it right over; when it has to plunge into horrible storms which seethe and leap, or contend with cross seas, a boat that does not right itself when overturned is only a lifeboat so long as it can maintain its proper position in the water.

The conventional carriage-launched lifeboat has developed over time, together with operational practices. Both are now well established. The carriage has changed little over the last 150 years. The RNLI's strategic plan required all offshore lifeboats to be fast and self-righting by 1993. This caused the traditional lifeboat design to be closely scrutinised. New tests resulted in the building of an experimental prototype to evaluate boat performance: launching off the carriage into the sea; recovery from the sea onto the beach; return to the carriage.

Mr F. D. Hudson was a naval architect with the firm Richard Dunston's of Hessle, East Yorkshire, before joining the RNLI. In 1983 he headed the RNLI's design team who were given the task of designing the F.C.B. (fast carriage boat.) The design considerations were: a 37- to 38-foot lifeboat, expected to have a speed of 16 knots, and to be self-righting with inherent buoyancy contained in a watertight wheelhouse and hull. The wheelhouse was to give protection to the six-man crew as well as all the electronic equipment – radio, radar, laser plotter, navigator – now standard fittings in all new lifeboats. The equipment had proved successful in the larger Arun and Tyne class lifeboats of the RNLI fleet. Many secondary requirements were also sought. The boat had to be compatible with existing carriages and had to fit into the existing lifeboat houses around the coast. The boat was developed, in house, entirely by RNLI staff; the requirements made the team look away from the conventional lifeboat design. The keel was laid down in 1986 and built by aluminium shipbuilders of Portchester, Portsmouth. The hull was then fitted out at William Osborne's of Littlehampton, Sussex and launched ready for trials in July 1987. After extensive trials the prototype boat was taken around the coast to let the crew handle it in all weathers, providing feedback from the men who were to operate this fleet of lifeboats when built. The outstanding success of the trials and all the positive feedback from the crews around the coast, convinced the RNLI's committee that the prototype aluminium boat, called 001, was fit for use as a lifeboat on station.

All prototype boat hulls, in the past, had only been used to improve design and were then scrapped. Lifeboat 001 was allocated to Bridlington in November 1988. It is RNLI tradition that each different class of offshore lifeboat, in the RNLI fleet, is named after an English river. This was to be named the Mersey class of lifeboats. The lifeboat's official number was 12-001; the first number of any lifeboat is its length, this boat was 12 metres long; the second set of numbers refers to lifeboats that have been built in the class. So this lifeboat was 12 metres long and the first one of its class to be built.

The Mersey class lifeboat had been designed and developed by the RNLI staff, for stations where the lifeboat had to be launched into the sea from a carriage. The Mersey has a speed of 16.5 knots, twice as fast as the old Oakley class lifeboat they were replacing.

The *Peggy and Alex Caird* was con-

29. *The* Peggy and Alex Caird *exercising in Bridlington Bay with helicopter from RAF Leconfield.*

structed of aluminium and was manned by a crew of six: coxswain, second coxswain, mechanic, second mechanic and two crewmen. She was designed to give easy access to machinery and reasonably low freeboard for recovering survivors, while keeping enough height in the bow for good sea keeping as well as preventing too much spray from covering the lifeboat in rough weather. The hull incorporates tunnels to give protection to the propellers in shallow water. In the event of capsize, the inherent buoyancy of her watertight wheelhouse enables her to self-right in six seconds. The wheelhouse contains seating for the crew of six and an additional seat for a doctor, together with the steering position, radar display, chart table, navigational aids, M.F. and VHF radio transmitter and receivers, and lockers containing an assortment of all the equipment needed for search and rescue operations.

The boat's specifications: length 38 feet, beam 12 feet 6 inches, depth 6 feet, draught 3 feet 2 inches, engines two Caterpillar 3208T turbo-charged marine diesels, fuel capacity 245 gallons of diesel at 16.5 knots, and a range of 145 nautical miles at full speed.

During February 1988 lifeboat trials with a new £574,084 prototype carriage-launch lifeboat took place at Bridlington, shortly after which the RNLI announced that Bridlington was to receive the first of the latest model of lifeboat in November that year. The new boat was the 12-metre Mersey class lifeboat, with which the lifeboat crew had been carrying out extensive lifeboat trials in Bridlington Bay and on the South Beach.

This was the start of a new chapter in the history of Bridlington lifeboat and for the first time moving away from the conventional lifeboat design.

An appeal was immediately launched for funds with which to extend the boathouse, originally built in 1903, in which to house the most modern hi-tech lifeboat in the country.

The new lifeboat was to be called the *Peggy and Alex Caird* after the late Miss Mildred Caird, of Glen Coe Street, Hull, who left £459,000 in her will to the RNLI. Peggy had spent many happy holidays in Bridlington and had strong links with the sea through her brother, Alex, who was a merchant seaman.

During the summer the station was fortunate enough to receive a £25,000 bequest from a Merseyside man, Richard Medlicott. This, combined with the £23,000 that had been raised from the generosity of the local community and friends of the station, enabled the boathouse alteration to commence without delay. Local contractors T.A. Hebden carried out the work. The main front door opening was raised and brought forward, and the two old wooden doors were replaced by one up-and-over door. Local system builders, Wiseplan, provided portable cabins for the crew to store their oilskins and other life-saving equipment, while the boathouse alterations took place. The cabins were sited down on the foreshore with kind permission of the council. This enabled the lifeboat and its crew still to be on call 24 hours a day during the building work. The work took three months and cost £47,000.

The huge increase in the cost of the *Peggy and Alex Caird* was due to her new technological design and build, together with the electronic equipment fitted into her lifeboat wheelhouses, which for the first time protected the delicate electronic systems from moisture and salt water.

Six crew-members attended the training centre at RNLI headquarters in Poole in Dorset for the first-ever Mersey class lifeboat sea training course, on Monday, 21 November 1988. The course was to train us to man and operate the new Mersey class lifeboat, working efficiently with the highly technical equipment, on service in all weather conditions.

The week's course moved from a conventional lifeboat with a speed of eight knots, to the most up-to-date lifeboat in the world with twice the speed of its predecessor. A major change for the crew was the wheelhouse where the crew could seek shelter and work protected from the weather. The crew became more efficient and able to work longer in search and rescue conditions. I remember commenting at the time that it was like flying on Concorde after flying in a Spitfire. Part of the week's training course was the return passage to Bridlington, due to leave from Poole late on Friday evening. This I insisted on delaying until one minute past midnight, Saturday 26 November 1988, once again because of fishermen's superstition: 'Never start anything new on a Friday'.

Setting off from Poole, we undertook a night passage to Newhaven, where we stayed only long enough for breakfast and to refuel. We then made a sea passage to Lowestoft and Grimsby, arriving in Bridlington on the morning of 28 November 1988. A large cheering crowd on the harbour top was waiting to welcome us, together with a flotilla of small vessels and the explosions of four lifeboat maroons. The new lifeboat *Peggy and Alex Caird* by tradition was escorted into the harbour by the *William Henry and Mary King*, the lifeboat she was to replace. After 17 days of intensive training, launching every evening and weekend to train the rest of the crew and helpers, the *Peggy and Alex Caird* was officially put on station by the RNLI ready for service at 6.19 p.m. on 15 December 1988.

The Lifeboat *Peggy and Alex Caird*

The naming and christening of the *Peggy and Alex Caird* took place on Saturday 17 June 1989 on Princess Mary Promenade. Crowds packed the area to watch the ceremony to which 600 guests had been invited.

Dr Terry Wilson, chairman of the Bridlington RNLI, opened the proceedings, mentioning that this lifeboat was the first for 41 years to be named in Bridlington. The lifeboat was then officially handed over to the RNLI by Mr C. Fincham on behalf of the executors of the late Miss M. Caird. The RNLI director, Lt Cdr Brian Miles RD, MNI, RNR, officially accepted the lifeboat saying, 'It is a historic day for the RNLI, this being the first Mersey class lifeboat'. Mr A. Edwards, Honorary Secretary, Bridlington station, accepted the lifeboat on behalf of the station. The Rev. John Meek then led the service of dedication. Miss J. Chippindale, Chairman of Bridlington Ladies Lifeboat Guild, proposed a vote of thanks.

Dr Terry Wilson invited Mary, Lady Macdonald of Sleat, President of the Ladies Lifeboat Guild, to name the lifeboat the *Peggy and Alex Caird*, breaking a 100-year-old bottle of champagne over the boat. The champagne had been presented to the station by Mr Tony Ellis, district staff officer of the Humber coastguard. Undrinkable, it had been passed down in the family to await an event of significance at which to use it.

Bridlington became the focus of many lifeboat crews from around the country. During the first year of operations *Peggy and Alex Caird*, was launched every weekend and during the week for lifeboat crews to visit and inspect the new Mersey class lifeboat. Lifeboat crews came with the sole intention of deciding whether the lifeboat was suitable for their station. With a few exceptions she became a firm favourite.

In 1989 she was launched on 62 occasions, of which 46 were for training and publicity purposes. During one such training exercise for publicity a local paper reported: 'My knuckles were white, as my hands gripped the rail in front of me when we surged forward; this was no fairground ride but the journey made by lifeboat men whenever a boat is in peril near Bridlington. In summer, conditions are bearable but in the middle of a howling gale force 10 wind in midwinter, conditions are not only diabolical but these men put their lives at risk to save others.' The weather at the time of the reporter's trip on board the lifeboat was wind west, force 3 to 4, and sea state moderate with good visibility.

The speed of the new lifeboat was demonstrated on 15 January 1989 when a windsurfer was seen from the shore clinging to his sailboard totally exhausted in a westerly force 8 gale, one mile east of South Cliff. The coastguards activated the lifeboat crew's paging system; eight minutes later the boat was launched and in four minutes the windsurfer, Geoff Hills, a 30-year-old man from Doncaster, was safely on board the lifeboat. He was then taken into the harbour where a coastguard mobile rescue unit was waiting to take him to hospital suffering from hypothermia. Twelve minutes from the crew alert to the rescue!

30. *The* Peggy and Alex Caird, *1990.*

The next two services were also for windsurfers in difficulty on 29 January and 6 February 1989.

On 9 February 1989, the *Peggy and Alex Caird* was taken through the town to the Priory Church. As part of the Great Gale service, the Rev. John Meek blessed the new lifeboat. This revived the old tradition of taking the lifeboat each year to the service. In the 1950s this had stopped, from difficulties caused by snow and ice as the boats increased in weight.

On 8 June 1989 the Humber coast–guards requested the lifeboat launch to assist a Dutch yacht unsure of its position in thick fog some 10 miles east-south-east of Flamborough Head. On launching the sea was calm, there was no wind and thick fog restricted our visibility to less than 50 yards. The new equipment on board the *Peggy and Alex Caird*, the VHF Radio direction finder, enabled the lifeboat to get a direct bearing on the radio signal transmitted by the Dutch yacht, and radar gave us the distance between the casualty and ourselves. We were able to pinpoint the casualty without difficulty. The yacht was to the south of the position he had reported to the coastguards. After going alongside, who had torn sails, auxiliary engine failure and was unsure of his position, we towed the yacht safely back into Bridlington Harbour.

This service was carried out with relative ease, thanks to the modern highly technical equipment now fitted in the Bridlington lifeboat. Gone are the days when services like this were like looking for a needle in a haystack, spending many hours' straining your eyes until they were red with salt spray, looking into a blanket of fog.

On 17 August 1990 the Humber coastguards informed the Honorary Secretary that a RAF Tornado aircraft was missing, thought to have crashed into the sea, and requested the lifeboat to carry out a search. We launched and made best possible speed to the first position given, arriving at 3.05 a.m. We searched the area given by the coastguards, eventually meeting up with the Skegness and Humber lifeboats. Eight other vessels also joined in the search, together with helicopters and fixed wing aircraft.

Coxswain Superintendent Brian W. Bevan of the Humber lifeboat, my old friend with whom I had worked on search and rescue operations many times, was nominated on-scene commander, surface search. All vessels were formed into line abreast and we commenced a box search. At 7.00 a.m. an oil slick and small pieces of wreckage were sighted. After searching the area thoroughly the three lifeboats and other vessels were released from the search at 11.45 a.m. by the coastguards. We returned to station at 2.30 p.m.

Though this service had been unsuccessful in saving lives, it highlighted how efficiently the search and rescue missions off the Yorkshire coast are carried out. The co-operation between the three lifeboats, eight other vessels, helicopters and fixed wing aircraft of the RAF was all co-ordinated from the Humber coastguard station at Bridlington.

A message from the Commanding Officer at RAF Pitreavie was received the following day: 'I am grateful for the immediate response to the call for assistance and the tremendous effort that went into the search for survivors and recovery of wreckage following the aircraft accident off the Yorkshire coast. Both S.A.R. (search and rescue) operations demonstrated how well we can work together and complement each other in time of crisis. Your professionalism and co-operation are much appreciated.'

The members of the Royal Yorkshire Yacht Club have been staunch supporters of the Bridlington lifeboat over many years. They have an impeccable record of safety, with the most stringent safety rules in place.

The elements can still catch out the most experienced seamen. On 9 August 1991 the J24 yacht *Jedi* was sailing in the Royal Yorkshire Yacht Club annual regatta. The wind was blowing force 7-8 westerly, when *Jedi* was caught by a strong gust of wind, which first broached the yacht and then she capsized throwing the crew of five into the water. Both the inshore and offshore lifeboats were immediately launched. The inshore lifeboat picked up all five of the yacht crew from the water. The offshore lifeboat managed to get hold of the yacht, which had sunk, raising it and towing it safely back into harbour.

On 30 May 1993 the J24 yacht *Just about Right* capsized in choppy seas, a victim of the force 7 gale that was blowing. They were seen from the Humber coastguard headquarters at Limekiln Lane. The lifeboat was immediately launched. The local fishing boat, *Eva Ann*, was close by the casualty, picking up the crew and taking them all safely into harbour. The lifeboat crew was able to get a rope on to the yacht, which again had sunk, and managed to right the boat before putting crew-member Andrew Brompton on board to helm the yacht as we towed her back into harbour.

1991 was a record year for lives saved by Bridlington lifeboats. The inshore lifeboat launched 45 times; the offshore lifeboat launched 19 times: 38 lives saved. In 1992 the offshore lifeboat was called out 28 times and the inshore lifeboat 30 times: 35 lives saved. These were the busiest two years in the history of Bridlington lifeboat.

Whilst the launching tractor was being overhauled in December 1994, the lifeboat was moored in the harbour; she was then available if an emergency call came. The lifeboat mooring chain snapped during a heavy storm, only hours after we had been out on a 12-hour service call to help a Dutch cargo vessel which had lost its rudder five miles east of Hornsea. As a result of the broken mooring chain, the lifeboat sustained slight damage to her aluminium hull, when she had been buffeted against the North Pier. A lifeboat from the reserve fleet, the *Marine Engineer*, was sent to Bridlington and put on service while the *Peggy and Alex Caird* was repaired at Grimsby.

Because of her prototype construction and hard trials she had undertaken before becoming a station lifeboat, 12:001 was taken back to shipyards on numerous occasions to strengthen her aluminium hull. It was decided by the RNLI after repairing the *Peggy and Alex Caird* that she should go into the reserve fleet. The new Bridlington lifeboat was to be the Mersey class lifeboat *Marine Engineer*.

The Lifeboat *Marine Engineer*

The present Bridlington offshore lifeboat is called *Marine Engineer*. The Institute of Marine Engineers is a professional institute and learned society, which celebrated its centenary in 1989. It has over 16,000 members in 80 countries and provides a full range of technical and other services to its members throughout the maritime industries. In order to mark the centenary in a way that would make a lasting contribution to the community, the Institute launched an appeal, amongst its members, to buy a Mersey class lifeboat for the RNLI. The *Marine Engineer*, was mainly funded in this way, with additional funding coming from the bequests of Elizabeth Barnett, Stewart Doris, Allen Cureton Willdigg and a gift from Mr Kenneth Street and his sister Mrs Vera Davis, in memory of their parents.

On 25 April 1991 at the Docklands sailing centre, Isle of Dogs, London HRH The Duchess of Kent named the *Marine Engineer*. The Docklands had been the RNLI store yard from 1882-1939, and the Institute of Marine Engineers was founded in east London in 1889. Following the introductions Lt Cdr Brian Miles, chairman of the RNLI (a great friend of Bridlington lifeboat station) thanked all those who had contributed to the appeal and the President of the Institute of Marine Engineers; Rear Admiral Michael Vallis also thanked his members throughout the world for their help. Mr Michael Vernon, chairman of the RNLI, formally accepted the lifeboat on behalf of the Institution. The service of dedication followed, conducted by the Rt. Rev. John Klyberg, Bishop of Fulham, with music by the Salvation Army band. The Duchess of Kent spoke of her respect and affection for the RNLI an affinity, which had grown since childhood visits to Yorkshire lifeboat stations. At that time the Duchess was not to know that the lifeboat she was naming would go on service at Bridlington on the Yorkshire coast some years later. With glowing acclaim the duchess pushed the lever to cause the foredeck to be awash with champagne and named the lifeboat *Marine Engineer*, shortly after which she went on board the lifeboat for a short sail around the Isle of Dogs.

The *Marine Engineer* was to go into the reserve fleet, to be used at lifeboat stations when their own boat was undergoing minor repairs, painting or a full refit, which each lifeboat undergoes every five years, to keep up-to-date and, as technology moves on, to be fitted with new equipment. This gives the lifeboat crews the best equipment possible with which to save lives at sea.

The *Marine Engineer* returned to the town to become the new Bridlington lifeboat on 12 August 1995 to be welcomed by the *Peggy and Alex Caird*, before leaving to join the reserve fleet.

On 23 September 1995 the service of rededication was held for the *Marine Engineer* in front of the inshore lifeboat house. A large crowd of people watched Colonel Iain R. Bryce open the proceedings, after which the Rev. Canon John Meek, Rector of Bridlington Priory and chaplain to the Bridlington lifeboat station, conducted the service of Re-Dedication of the Mersey class lifeboat *Marine Engineer*. Music was provided by the Bridlington Excelsior Band.

The hull of the *Marine Engineer* is built of fibre-reinforced composite, which combines strength with light weight. Its length is 38 feet, beam 12 feet 6 inches, depth 6 feet, draught 3 feet 2 inches. Like its predecessor it has fully protected propellers, needed when working in shallow water. She is self-righting and the two Caterpillar 3208T turbo charged marine diesel engines provide a speed of 16 knots, with a range of 145 miles; she carries a crew of six. The superstructure houses the watertight wheelhouse. Entry is by the watertight door on the after end at

31. *Launching today's Lifeboat, the* Marine Engineer.

the port side. Inside the wheelhouse a second watertight door gives access to the engine room. Moving through the engine room, another watertight door leads into a small survivors' cabin, which contains a bench seat down either side, lockers for equipment, spare ropes etc. The cradle stretcher, which is carried by the lifeboat, is secured on the starboard side. At the forward end of this cabin is the main locker for the anchor cable, which feeds, when in use, through the deck head (roof of the cabin) and onto the foredeck. Inside the wheelhouse is the coxswain's or helmsman's seat; this is on the port side forward, in front of which is the steering wheel with engine controls. To the right-hand side, in front of this position, is the compass at eye level and indicators linked to the engine with fire-warning lights. Overhead the display includes an echo sounder and automatic VHF radio directional finder. On the forward right-hand side of the wheelhouse is the second coxswain's seat, in front of which is the radar set; behind this position is the chart table and mechanic's seat with the radio sets and the latest global positional satellite navigation equipment. Behind the coxswain's seat are fitted two seats for other crew-members; the third crew-member seat is aft of the mechanic's position. Under these seats are lockers containing all the equipment needed by the lifeboat crew. The lifeboat carries a comprehensive first-aid kit, including entinox and oxygen, for use on casualties. The water heater for hot drinks is on the port side just inside the watertight entry door. Back on deck, at the aft end of the superstructure is the outside steering position. The second steering wheel, compass and many of the instruments are duplicated from the inside instrument panel. This position is used when going alongside in the harbour or a vessel at sea. During this operation this steering position gives the coxswain/helmsman better all-round vision. Above this position is the mast structure which holds the radar scanner, VHF radio direction-finding aerials, navigation lights, and flag signal halyards. This mast is hinged and lowered onto the after deck, when the lifeboat is housed. In the deck of the upper steering position is a small hatch, which gives access to the emergency steering gear. Around the deck of the lifeboat are guard rails for the crew's protection, but designed in such a way that if they are snagged or catch onto anything they will easily break away without damaging the hull of the lifeboat. Fitted onto the forward end of the superstructure are two large rope bins. On the foredeck the two anchors are stowed and a small single-barrel winch is fitted to the centre of the foredeck. Two 18-foot radio aerials are fitted to the wheelhouse coach roof, which are lowered parallel to the deck when re-housing the lifeboat.

I requested permission from the RNLI for the East Riding Yorkshire Rose to be painted on the stern of the new lifeboat; permission was granted. This welcoming rose greets anyone now entering the Bridlington lifeboat station.

Although *Marine Engineer* launched several times on service while she was station at Bridlington as a reserve lifeboat, the first service launch as the Bridlington lifeboat was on 22 August 1995. The Bridlington fishing boat *Castle Bay* alerted the coastguards when it developed gearbox trouble in dense fog 35 miles east of Flamborough Head. The coastguards requested the *Marine Engineer* to launch to go to the aid of the casualty. The fishing boat had a crew of five; visibility was down to less than 200 yards. The poor visibility proved no problem to the lifeboat, which with its satellite location equipment is able to pinpoint vessels in difficulty to within 30 feet. Within

32. *Launching today's Lifeboat, the* Marine Engineer.

33-36. *Today's Lifeboat*, Marine Engineer, *on exercise.*

three hours the lifeboat had towed the vessel safely into Bridlington harbour.

On 18 June 1998 the coastguards alerted the lifeboat crew, asking for an immediate lifeboat launch. An F. 3 Tornado aircraft based at RAF Coningsby in Lincolnshire had disappeared from the radar screen while on a training flight. On launching we were informed that the Filey lifeboat, Sea King helicopters from Leconfield and RAF Bulmer together with a Nimrod fixed wing aircraft were joining the search for the missing Tornado. We launched at 1.30 p.m. and arrived on scene at 3.00 p.m. Together with Filey lifeboat we carried out a search of the area, widening the search pattern continually. The fog increased in density, visibility was down below 50 yards, which made the search very difficult, and crew-members of the lifeboat were on deck throughout this time. The helicopters had to be stood down from the search because visibility was so poor. After a search lasting just short of seven hours, in which small pieces of wreckage were recovered from the scene, both Bridlington and Filey lifeboats were stood down from the search and returned to station. The whole rescue operation had been co-ordinated by the Humber coastguards and staff at RAF Kinloss in Scotland.

Once again the modern technology on board both lifeboats enabled the search for the missing aircraft and pilot to take place in hazardous weather conditions. Despite the thick fog the lifeboats were able to continue searching.

Today's Lifeboat Tractor

The lifeboat tractor station at Bridlington, used to launch the offshore lifeboat, is the first tractor to be specifically designed to launch lifeboats from carriages. Every one of its predecessors had been converted from commercial vehicles, which were becoming more costly to adapt, to meet the highest specifications required by the RNLI.

The Talus tractor was developed by the RNLI together with M.A. Bigland Ltd of Knighton, Powys, Wales, where its development took place. The prototype was taken and tested at various lifeboat stations under the most arduous launching conditions. At the conclusion of these trials, which were very successful, one of the first tractors was sent to Bridlington. It weighs 17.5 tonnes, length 18 feet 6 inches, width 8 feet, height 9 feet 6 inches, power 200 hp diesel engine, which gives it a top speed of 9 miles per hour, with the ability to pull a weight of 15 tonnes. A winch is fitted at the rear of the vehicle, which will also pull 15 tonnes; it has a cab for the driver, which is fully waterproof. On the top of the cab are fitted two floodlights to illuminate the working area, when on the beach during the hours of darkness. The driver's seat can face either way. The driver controls the vehicle by a 'Joy stick' which is pushed in the direction of the travel required. Power to the joystick is controlled by a dead man's foot pedal which is the only control necessary for the movement of the vehicle, other than engine speed. The winch is operated from inside the cab by a lever, again protected by a dead man's pedal.

On 18 October 2000 the coastguards activated the crew pagers at 4.56 a.m., asking us to launch to the fishing boat *Diana* who was in difficulty aground to the south of Bridlington. At the launch site the wind was south force 7 with a rough sea, heavy south-east swell with rain. As we pushed into the water to launch, the breaking swells were cracking over the tractor. As the chains, which held the lifeboat onto the carriage, were released the lifeboat was pushed by the surging waves back two to three feet on the carriage. The tractor driver, Ken Smith, realised what was happening and from experience sounded the hooter on the tractor and reversed quickly towards the shore, providing the lifeboat with the momentum to launch off the carriage.

On arrival at the casualty we found the boat was aground, bow facing the cliffs, 20 yards north of Barmston drain, a large concrete structure running across the beach east to west, four miles south of Bridlington. The wind was south-east force 7, and the *Diana* was being driven up the sandy beach by heavy swell and the flowing tide. In-shore from his position was the rock formation, which protects the landward end of Barmston drain. The skipper was worried that they were being driven towards these rocks. The lifeboat manoeuvred close to the casualty, operating sometimes in less than six feet of water, with the lifeboat keel striking the bottom several times. A heaving line was eventually passed and then a nylon towrope was passed across to the casualty. During this time the casualty and lifeboat were being constantly covered by breaking seas. The lifeboat was pushed to the north by the swell and the wind, and had to be constantly repositioned, quite a task in shallow water with the towrope connected to the casualty, but with great teamwork this was done several times. We gradually took the strain on the towrope, inch by inch the *Diana*'s bow came round to face the east, and eventually we managed to pull her clear of the beach and into deeper water. After seeing the *Diana* safely alongside in Bridlington Harbour the lifeboat returned to the beach, to re-carriage before returning to station.

Bridlington has witnessed significant change in the fishing industry over the past 10 years. From trawling for white fish, cod, haddock etc, to catching shell fish, crabs, lobsters and whelks, the fishing patterns have altered. Calls on the lifeboat today from the fishing fleet mainly come when mechanical failures occur, sometimes 30 to 40 miles from the safety of the harbour. The leisure side of boating also brings calls on the lifeboat from time to time: yachts passing along the coast, or local pleasure boats in need of help. Whenever the call for help is received the Bridlington lifeboat *Marine Engineer* stands ready.

The Inshore Lifeboat

To enable the RNLI to improve the rescue of people in small boats, 1962 saw the beginning of trials with small fast inflatable boats, ever mindful of the constantly changing use of the sea. Incidents happened short distances off the beach and coastline around the UK; speed of rescue was the main requirements from the inflatable boats. The conventional lifeboats, built to cope with the worst weather conditions, were not the ideal craft for going to the help of bathers, small boats or dinghy sailors who got into trouble on a summer's day. Few conventional lifeboats had the speed for this kind of rescue. As the trials and development advanced, the 'Inshore Rescue Boats,' as they were then called, were manufactured from a tough material proofed with neoprene, and a 40 b.h.p outboard engine was mounted on the wooden transom, which produced a speed of over 20 knots. She was 15 feet 9 inches long, 6 feet 3 inches beam, the weight was 295 lb, and she carried 12 gallons of fuel in two flexible tanks, giving the boat at full speed at least two hours' running time, without refuelling. The boat

37. The present lifeboat tractor with first driver Ken Smith.

came with a small two-wheel launching trailer.

Bridlington's first inshore rescue boat (the name was changed by the RNLI to inshore lifeboat in 1972) arrived in Bridlington in April 1966. Training for the crews on the new lifeboat commenced immediately. After eight weeks, on 2 June 1966 the I.R.B. was exercised, the crew demonstrating to Commander L. Hill, the district inspector of lifeboats, that they were competent to operate the boat safely if it were needed in an emergency. At the close of the exercise Commander Hill declared the I.R.B. 'D-92' fully operational during the summer months to cover the area from Thornwick Bay in the north to Withernsea in the south and up to five miles offshore.

The I.R.B. carried a pair of oars, a compass fitted into the mattress, which covered the bottom of the boat, three stowage pockets for equipment, fire extinguisher, first-aid equipment, and an anchor with an anchor rope and chain. An agreement was reached with the RAF that, until a permanent boathouse could be found, the boat would be kept in the RAF hanger on Gummers Wharf (now Rag's Restaurant). Launching took place down the slipway at the landward end of the South Pier. Later it was transferred to the north side of the main lifeboat house, and today the site of the souvenir shop. In 1967 it was again on the move, this time to the south end of a rain shelter on

Princess Mary Promenade, only 50 yards from the beach. The Bridlington Corporation, who generously footed the £250 costs for that work, undertook the planning for the first inshore lifeboat house, together with its conversion.

On 31 May 1967, just under one year after the boat was made operational, Cdr L. Hill returned to Bridlington to receive the keys to the new boathouse from Councillor A.C. Dunn, chairman of the Bridlington foreshores committee.

During the same year (1967), Bridlington I.R.B. and eight other inshore stations were fitted with experimental VHF radio equipment, enabling them to keep in touch with the coastguards and helicopters. These experiments proved a great success, considering the environment and conditions in which the radios were to be used. As a result of the successful trials the RNLI supplied its fleet of I.R.B.s around the coastline of the United Kingdom with these radios. As time and technology has moved forward, modifications and improvements have been constantly made to the equipment carried by these boats. From 1967 to 1999 the inshore lifeboat was only on service for the summer months, from April through until October, when it was withdrawn for servicing and refitting. From 1999, because of the improved equipment the boat carried together with the improved dry suits the RNLI now issued as standard for all inshore lifeboat crews, the I.L.B. was put on service for the full 12 months of the year.

During the first seven years in which the inshore lifeboat was stationed at Bridlington, the boat was manhandled and pushed, on a small launching carriage, from the boathouse down the slipway across the beach to the water's edge to be launched. In May 1973 a second-hand Fordson agricultural tractor was purchased by the crew, through the generosity of the people of Bridlington and the fund-raising activities of the lifeboat crews club. The tractor helped to speed up the launching of the I.R.B., which if the sand was soft and the tide out had been a very strenuous task, but by the end of the summer season we had the fittest lifeboat crew in the history of the station. The tractor was replaced by a four-wheel-drive Mercedes *Unimog*, supplied by the RNLI in 1983. In 1986 this vehicle was in turn changed for a Ford agricultural tractor, which in 1994 was replaced with a reconditioned tractor with hydraulics at a cost of £7,200 plus VAT, and in February 2004 this was superseded by a reconditioned Fordson Major agricultural tractor. The agricultural tractor has been the ideal vehicle for moving the inshore lifeboat across the wide-open beach, which we have at low water. The tractor also doubles as the vehicle used to move the cart, on which the offshore lifeboat's beach recovery gear is stored, which is kept at the inshore lifeboat house, as it is not needed until the offshore lifeboat returns to the beach after a service launch or exercise.

All inshore lifeboats have an operational number similar to those of the offshore lifeboats, which follow the letter 'D', the 'D' class of lifeboat.

D-92 was provided from funds of the institution.

D-188 was funded by a gift of £1,000 from Hucknall Round Table, Nottinghamshire. The proceeds had come from a carnival held by them. The boat was handed over to the station in May 1971 by Mr J. Greenhalgh, chairman of Hucknall Round Table and accepted by Dr T. Wilson, chairman of the Bridlington RNLI.

D-299's cost was defrayed by a gift from the Lords Feoffees and Assistants of the Manor of Bridlington. The inshore lifeboat was handed over to the station by the Chief Lord, Mr. B. Rogers. The ceremony was held on the forecourt of the offshore

38. *An exercise launch of the first IRB down the slipway from the harbour, May 1966. Note the lightweight oilskins and lack of footwear.*

39. *The first IRB boathouse on Princess Mary's Promenade with the inshore boat and tractor, 1993.*

40. *Chief Lord Brian Rogers with president of the station William Pinkney and chairman of the Branch committee Dr Terry Wilson at the naming ceremony of the Lords Feoffees inshore boat, 10 June 1984.*

41. *Left to right: Crew-members Mark Crozier, Grant Walkington, Adrian Trower onboard the* Lords Feoffees III *at her naming ceremony. Note the lifejackets, drysuits and helmets now used by the ILB crews.*

42. Today's inshore lifeboat, Lords Feoffees III, *ready to launch.*

43. Crew launching the Lords Feoffees III.

44. Crewman Mark Crozier preparing and starting the engine.

45. *Inshore lifeboat* Lords Feoffees III *launched on exercise.*

lifeboat house on 10 June 1984. The boat was received on behalf of the station by Mr W. Pinkney and Dr T. Wilson, President and Chairman of Bridlington RNLI respectively.

During 1992 plans were drawn up for the first purpose-built inshore lifeboat house in Bridlington, on Princess Mary's Promenade. The building was to incorporate changing facilities, a drying-room area, crew room, an office in which the Honorary Secretary could carry out his duties, and a small souvenir shop. This custom-built building, which cost £60,000, replaced the old shelter conversion which had served as the inshore lifeboat house for many years. On 2 October 1993 the opening of the building and the naming ceremony of the new inshore lifeboat D-426, which again had been generously funded by the Lords Feoffees, took place at the inshore lifeboat house. The ceremony was witnessed by a large crowd of crew and supporters; and the proceedings were opened by Chairman of the Bridlington Branch, Iain Bryce. There followed a short service led by the Rev. John Meek, rector of the Priory Church. The Chief Lord of the Manor of Bridlington, Mr B. Rogers, then named the boat *Lords Feoffees II*; the champagne for this task was donated by local man Simon Williams.

D-557 was the third inshore lifeboat to be generously donated to the station by the town's ancient charity, the Lords Feoffees. On Sunday, 17 September 2000, following the official opening, the Chief Lord of the Manor of Bridlington, Mr B. Gray, handed over the new lifeboat to the RNLI. Mr Gilbert Gray QC, a member of the RNLI's committee of management, accepted the boat. This was followed by a service of dedication, conducted by the Rev. John Wardle, rector of Bridlington Priory Church. Mr B. Gray then named the lifeboat, pouring champagne across the bows of the *Lords Feoffees III*.

The Lords Feoffees and their Assistants of the Manor of Bridlington are an elected body, having been in existence for upwards of four centuries. They are a registered charity, administering property in the Manor of Bridlington and disbursing their funds for the good of the town.

In 1808 the Lords Feoffees donated £5 and 5 shillings towards the repair of the Bridlington lifeboat after damage had been sustained. Unfortunately the details of this damage and how it was caused have been lost in the passage of time.

In more recent times the generous funding of the inshore lifeboats, *Lords Feoffees, I, II* and *III*, has enabled the inshore lifeboat crews to save the lives of many people.

7

The Medal and Vellum
Certificate Services

During the early years of the lifeboat services, life along the coast still relied on 'free traders' (smugglers). It was not uncommon for communities to believe that wrecks were heaven sent for plunder; survivors from wrecked vessels were unwelcome and possibly embarrassing. Superstition also played a part and people believed that certain punishment awaited anyone foolish enough to interfere with the sea's natural toll in human life. In spite of this, lives in danger from the sea were saved and deeds of heroism performed by men and women of all social backgrounds, from the shore, with nothing to gain but self-respect and the knowledge that they had done their duty.

At the first general meeting of the Royal National Institution for the Preservation of Life from Shipwreck, on 4 March 1824, the second resolution moved by W. Wilberforce Esq., MP for Hull, and seconded by Capt. Deans Dundas, RN, was that medallion and pecuniary rewards were to be given to those who rescued lives in cases of shipwreck. Since that time, after each launch or practice small monetary rewards have been made to lifeboat crews. The RNLI awards medals and inscriptions on vellum for outstanding gallant deeds. Initially there were only two medals, a Gold or Silver. In February 1917 the committee of management decided to institute a Bronze Medal. It made possible the decoration of men for services, which, though distinguished, would not earn the Gold or Silver Medal. These decorations are recognised as a token of a noble act – that of saving life – and are greatly appreciated and highly prized by the recipients and coveted by men of all classes.

For many years the medals carried a bust of the sovereign, but, when George VI came to the throne, it was made known that the king's likeness was to appear on medals only awarded personally by His Majesty. In 1938 the design of the RNLI medal was changed to show the bust of Lt Col Sir William Hillary, Bt., founder of the RNLI. On the reverse of the medals, since 1824, is the design by Mr William Wyon (1795-1851) of the Royal Mint, from a sketch by Henry Howard RA (1796-1847), depicting three men in a lifeboat, one of whom is in the act of rescuing an exhausted man from the sea. It is inscribed with the words, 'Let not that the deep swallow me up,' which is adapted from the Bible, Psalm 69, verse 15, 'Let not the water flood overflow me, neither the deep swallow me up.' The medal is suspended from a blue-corded silk ribbon from a bar formed by two dolphins, their heads facing.

The RNLI Gold Medal is awarded for an act in which outstanding courage; skills and initiative have been shown together with exceptional courage. The RNLI Silver Medal is for an outstanding act of merit, and the RNLI Bronze Medal for an act of conspicuous gallantry and courage.

We must be aware that these awards are made by the RNLI for the saving of life and are not restricted to the saving of life through the use of a lifeboat. However, because of the circumastances in which most life-saving rescues are carried out, 99.99 per cent of awards are made to lifeboat crews.

The RNLI distibuted handbills in the 1870s to boatmen and others to encourage prompt and energetic actions in times of danger to save life around the coasts of the British Isles, either by shore boats or other means. The RNLI grants rewards of money or medals. These rewards are given without further delay than is necessary to obtain proof of the merits of each case and to insure payment to the right parties.

The *Fox*

The first award given by the RNLI to a Bridlington man was to John Usher, landlord of the *Tiger Inn* (today the same building is the *George* public house, overlooking the harbour), who was at the same time the volunteer coxswain of the Bridlington Quay lifeboat.

Up to 1827, like many businessmen, he had been a part owner of a sailing ship, which had been involved in the coastal trade: the *John*, built on the river Hull in 1799 and then registered at Bridlington Quay in 1819.

The rescue took place before detailed records were kept. The RNLI recorded that the award was made for the rescue by lifeboat. On 10 January 1828, in a tremendous gale, heavy seas and a blizzard with snow two feet deep on the sand at low tide, the Montrose schooner *Fox*, on passage from Pillau, East Prussia, to Yarmouth with a cargo of linseed, was driven ashore south of Bridlington. Three apprentices who launched the ship's boat before the arrival of the lifeboat were drowned. Although it was by then dark and conditions extremely bad, the master, mate and one seaman were brought ashore to safety in the lifeboat.

Silver Medal awarded to **Coxswain John Usher**

The *Eagle*

On 24 October 1834, the Peterhead sloop *Eagle* was stranded on the beach near Bridlington during a severe storm. In attempting to launch the ship's small boat, it capsized and was carried away by the violent breaking seas. On seeing this, Mr George Gray rode into the surf on a horse and manage to pass a rope to the sloop, this was tied to a heavier rope, which was then hauled to the shore. Mr Gray, after returning to the beach, dismounted and went back into the surf on foot. Holding the rope, he helped ashore the exhausted survivors, the master, a crew of four and one passenger, in spite of being buried by waves several times.

Silver Medal awarded to **George Gray**

Monetary awards were made to 10 other men who helped with the rescue, by means of lines, from the shore.

The Coble *Fly*

On 10 October 1865 the coble *Fly* capsized in a heavy sea in the entrance of Bridlington Harbour, while endeavouring to leave the safety of the harbour in order to reach the *Sarah Horn of Whitstable*, who had entered the Bay showing signalling that she was in need of immediate help. A Bridlington youth, Thomas Hopper Frankish, a seaman, was lowered over the side of the pier wall, with a life buoy round him. From the heavy confused sea that threatened constantly to dash him against the stone pier wall, he successfully managed to rescue a man, Stephen Postill, who had been floundering in the water. Without Thomas's actions the poor fellow would have undoubtedly perished. The crew of a boat managed to rescue three of the other five men who were lost out of the capsized coble, but had not been washed into such a dangerous position as the first man. The remaining two occupants of the coble *Fly* managed to get ashore and were saved.

The award was made in acknowledgement of Thomas's daring conduct.

Silver Medal awarded to **Thomas H. Frankish**
Thanks inscribed on parchment and £2.

£2 10s. 0d. was awarded to the coble's crew for rescuing three men, lost out of the capsized coble *Fly*.

The *Charlotte*

The award was as a result of an incident, which took place at nearby Flamborough, four years before the Flamborough lifeboat stations were established. Bridlington was the nearest lifeboat station to the incident. On 1 January 1867, the Sunderland brig *Charlotte* was wrecked during a strong north-east gale on East Scar, North Landing, Flamborough. James Harrington waded into the violent surf several times, despite the cold and risks, which resulted in saving the lives of four men of the crew.

The award to James Harrington was in recognition of his gallant conduct, at the risk of his own life.

Silver Medal awarded to **James Harrington**
He was also given £2.

Ten shillings was awarded to each of the two men who gave assistance during the rescue.

Capsized Rowing Boats

On 17 April 1890 a northerly gale suddenly blew up as Mr H. Hutchinson was returning to harbour in his coble. He had passengers on board whom he had taken into the Bay for a sail. He picked up a rowing boat, which was in great difficulties from the sudden change of weather. The men in the boat were unable to make any headway towards the harbour against the strong northerly wind and growing swell. Henry took the six occupants on board his coble and towed the small rowing boat behind his boat.

Shortly after this he saw two other rowing boats in difficulty, being blown away from the harbour by the storm. Both the boats capsized in a sudden squall. Lowering the sail of the coble and leaving his boat and passengers, he jumped into the small rowing boat he was towing. Summoning all his skill he rowed to the two men, who had been thrown into the water, and pulled them into the rowing boat and safety. Returning to his coble and passengers, he took the rescued men on board his coble, and then sailed back to harbour safely despite the difficult conditions.

The award to Henry Hutchinson was given for his remarkable presence of mind, skill and courage shown by him on this occasion.

Silver Medal awarded to **Henry Hutchinson**, fisherman.
With a framed copy of the vote inscribed on vellum and three and a half guineas.

The *Victoria*

By 19 November 1893 storm-force northerly winds had been blowing across the area for some days, causing many vessels, large and small, to shelter in Bridlington Bay. During the hours of darkness the wind increased and veered to the north-east, making the Bay less sheltered. As was the custom with many fishermen, Christopher 'Kit' Brown, knowing that many ships were anchored in the Bay, asked his son Fred to go to the harbour top to make sure all was safe with the ships in the Bay, before they turned in for the night. Just after 12.30 a.m. Fred returned from the harbour breathlessly telling his father that there was a vessel burning the distress signal close to the shore, just outside the shore breaks, which was thundering onto the beach. Immediately Christopher Brown and his son roused two other fishermen who lived nearby. Quickly they rushed to the harbour and on the way they met another fisherman, Tom Clark, who agreed to go with them. They manned the small 24-foot long coble *Swiftsure*, and the five fishermen in complete darkness left the harbour under a fully reefed main sail, running before the storm-force winds and heavy seas towards the *Victoria* of Aberdeen. As the coble rounded her stern, a signal flare illuminated the area, but there was no sign of life and it looked as though all hands had been lost. Bringing the coble up into the wind under the lee of the vessel, two of the fishermen jumped on board to carry out a search. The fishermen found five of the crew lying around the deck in various stages of exhaustion; the captain, transfixed and glassy-eyed, was still clutching the ship's wheel oblivious to his surroundings with his eyes fixed on the heavens. With great difficulty the survivors were transferred into the coble. Just as they were about to cast off from the wreck, one of them said that someone was still on board the *Victoria*, which appeared to be quickly sinking. Two of the fishermen boarded the wreck again to search for the missing crewman, and found the cook lying unconscious in the galley. They dragged him across the deck and passed him into the coble. Quickly the two fishermen jumped into the *Swiftsure*, hoisted the reefed sail, and cast off from the wreck setting course for the harbour. As very experienced fishermen they knew they were still in great danger. The coble was now facing the full violence of the wind and raging sea. On the outward journey they had to run before the weather. Now they had the daunting task of tacking back up into the wind and raging swell. Before they had gone 200 yards, the doomed wreck of the *Victoria* was struck by a series of heavy breakers, lurched heavily and disappeared under the thundering waves. Christopher 'Kit' Brown was on the tiller of the *Swiftsure* which was being bombarded by heavy seas and storm-force winds, together with snow and hail showers. Brown displayed exceptional seamanship as he steered the coble through the heavy north-easterly surf near the harbour entrance. Safely alongside, the five fishermen landed the exhausted crew of the *Victoria*. They were taken to the Waterloo Cafe, which had opened its doors in readiness to provide hot baths, a good hot meal and warm beds for their recovery, all paid for by the Shipwrecked Mariners Society.

Silver Medals and Board of Trade Silver Medals awarded to **Christopher Brown, Fred Brown, Thomas Clark, Richard Purvis** and **John Usher**.

All five recipients were also given monetary rewards from the RNLI, the board of trade and the people of Nottingham.

This was an outstanding act of bravery on the part of all five fishermen. But when we look at the actions of Richard Purvis, during this period of storm force weather on 18, 19 and 20 November 1893, I understand why he was held in such high esteem by so many of the community. On 18 November 1893 he was the crew-member on board the lifeboat *William John and Frances* launching at 10.00 a.m. On 19 November 1893 he was rescuing the crew of the *Victoria*. On 20 November 1893 he was a crew-member once again on board the lifeboat *William John and Frances* launching at 10.00 a.m. Another lifeboat crew-member on this launch was Thomas Clark. The accounts of 18 November and 20 November, along with the tragic death of Christopher Brown, can be found on pages 52 to 57.

M.F.V. *Normanby*

On 6 January 1967, at 5.40 p.m. a local fishing vessel, *Normanby* from Bridlington, was sending out a Mayday, which had been picked up by the coastguards. She was requesting immediate assistance, reporting that she had run aground somewhere between Flamborough Head and South Landing. The lifeboat was launched at 6.05 p.m. under the command of Coxswain John King. The launch had been hampered by very dangerous road conditions, because of heavy snowfall over the previous three hours. The tractor, boat and carriage had to be lowered down the slipway by rope. On launching the lifeboat, *Tillie Morrison, Sheffield II*, proceeded on the dead-reckoning course for North Buoy (this was before radar was fitted to lifeboats). Visibility was very poor, and there were snow showers, wind southerly force 4, with a slight swell. On reaching the estimated position, the lifeboat contacted the casualty by radio.

The lifeboat searched along the coastline, as close inshore as was safe, and illuminated the area with parachute flares. *Normanby* was eventually spotted, aground and lying on a rock scar, known as Dreaver Dock, rolling on the rocks with the motion of the sea, but not making water. The lifeboat dropped a kedge anchor and veered in to within 60 yards of the *Normanby*; the lifeboat was only in approximately nine feet of water. The crew of the *Normanby* refused to leave their ship. A Schermuly rocket line gun was fired twice by crew man George Traves to try to get a rope across to the casualty. Both had the range but both failed to hit the small target – she was laid head on to the cliff with only her stern showing. The wind was very turbulent under the cliff and the coastguards said it was essential that they got a line on board. The coxswain decided to reset the anchor in a better position, where the lifeboat could veer closer to the *Normanby*. In doing so the lifeboat touched the bottom several times, but managed to get close enough to get a line on board the casualty. The lifeboat then pulled off on the kedge anchored to a safer position and by doing so she was able to maintain the *Normanby*'s position and prevent her driving up the shore as the flowing tide came through. Eventually the lifeboat managed to pull the *Normanby* off the rock scar into deeper water and the crew of the *Normanby* could then start her engine. After the recovery of the anchor, the lifeboat accompanied her back to the safety of Bridlington Harbour. Visibility throughout the service had been very poor but was now down to around 50 yards in the heavy snow. Both vessels entered the harbour safely at 9.35 p.m. The lifeboat was left moored in the harbour all night because of ice and snow on the slipway. Overnight the council sanded and salted the slipway, which then enabled the lifeboat to be rehoused ready for service the following morning.

The award to John King was given for the meritorious conduct of coxswain and crew in such adverse weather conditions.

Thanks of the Institution inscribed on vellum to Coxswain **John E. King**.

The Vellum service certificates were awarded to the rest of the crew: **J. Simpson, D. Atkins, R. Stott, G. Traves, F. Walkington and B. Bevan**.

This was the first service launch of my very good friend Brian William Bevan, MBE, who later became Coxswain Superintendent of the Humber Lifeboat, the only man to be awarded RNLI's Gold, Silver and Bronze Medals in the same year.

Two Men Fall over cliff

On 26 March 1967, at 8.00 p.m. Bridlington Coastguard requested that the ILB be launched to assist Flamborough Lifeboat with the rescue of two youths, who had fallen down the cliffs at South Landing. As it was dark and the wind force 5 south-westerly with a very choppy sea, it was decided to launch both the ILB and the offshore lifeboat to act as a mother ship; the inshore lifeboat at this time was not equipped with a radio. Her Majesty's coastguard cliff team were on the beach with casualties. Once on the scene, the ILB made its way with great difficulty into the shore and quickly the coastguards helped get the two casualties on board the ILB. Then, turning her head to sea, the helmsman Harry Wood managed with great skill to get clear of the rough water close to the shore, making a course towards the lifeboat, as the sea conditions were quite bad. On coming alongside the offshore lifeboat, it was seen that one of the casualties had a broken leg; he had been strapped into a Neal Robertson stretcher, and was lying in the bottom of the ILB. Both casualties were transferred, under difficult conditions, to the offshore lifeboat. Both lifeboats then made their way back to Bridlington harbour where the casualties were landed into the safe hands of the waiting ambulance.

The award to Harry T. Wood was for the courage and determination displayed by him during this rescue.

Thanks of the Institution inscribed on vellum to helmsman **H.T. Wood.**

A framed letter of thanks was awarded to **Mr R. Cooper**, crew-member of the inshore lifeboat that night.

The *Maria F*

On 4 February 1968, at 4.00 p.m. the coaster *Maria F* of Hamburg, a regular visitor to Bridlington Harbour, with a cargo of fertiliser on board was dragging her anchor about one mile east by south of Bridlington harbour. There was 16 degrees of frost with snow and sleet falling, reducing visibility to half a mile. The *William Henry and Mary King* was launched under the command of Second Coxswain John (Jack) Simpson; John King was at that time out of town. The wind was blowing a strong south-east gale causing a rough sea. The *Maria F* was located half a mile from the harbour entrance. She was being pounded from stem to stern by heavy seas, and both her anchors were dragging, causing her to drift into the RAF mooring buoys, outside Bridlington harbour, fouling her propellers. There were lights on in the coaster wheelhouse where the crew could be seen, but no contact by radio or signal could be made because of the weather conditions. No one was seen on deck. The weather made it impossible to put a man from the lifeboat on board the vessel. At high water the lifeboat returned to the harbour to assess the situation with the Honorary Secretary. Coxswain King was now available. Following renewed gale warnings it was feared that the casualty would suffer damage to the hull at low water. Two further attempts were made by the lifeboat to make contact with the crew, but despite all efforts none could be made, and the lifeboat stayed with the vessel. Shortly after midnight the *Maria F* started pounding the seabed badly, on the ebbing tide, and she then sent out a visible distress signal. The lifeboat anchored and then veered down to the vessel with the engines in constant use. The lifeboat was ranging so much that it would have been dangerous for any survivors to jump with any certainty of landing on the lifeboat deck, as she was being laid on her beam ends by the pounding sea. Coxswain King decided to try an approach from a different angle, but while manoeuvring both propellers were fouled, leaving the lifeboat with her starboard quarter open to the weather and the cockpit being constantly filled by breaking seas. As a precaution they asked for the Flamborough lifeboat to be launched. The task of freeing the propellers then began and the crew provided a human barrier to prevent water entering the engine room, when the hatch was opened to gain access to the propeller-freeing tool. With this the crew managed slowly to cut the rope around the port propeller shaft, allowing the port engine to be used for the return to the beach to clear the starboard propeller of the remaining rope. At 2.50 a.m. the lifeboat was again launched, to help the *Maria F* and her crew. The Flamborough lifeboat had arrived on scene and stood by outside the broken water. As the lifeboat closed into the vessel, one of the crew requested to be taken off. Coxswain King manoeuvred the lifeboat as close as possible, whilst the lifeboat crew all stood on the starboard deck ready to catch the crew-member, a female cook. The lifeboat was pitching violently as the jump was made; she was caught by one of the crew-members on the starboard shoulder of the lifeboat. The motion of the boat threw her and the crew-member into the fore cockpit, resulting in the cook receiving a fractured arm and wrist. The other crew-members of the *Maria F* decided to stay on board. The lifeboat entered harbour with the injured woman who was taken to hospital by the waiting ambulance. The lifeboat returned to sea and stood by the vessel. Conditions improved through the rest of the night. At 8.30 a.m., the lifeboat took out from the harbour an English-speaking German master to talk with the *Maria F* crew. This resulted in the master of the coaster coming ashore in the lifeboat to contact the owners and arrange for the tug to tow the coaster away for repairs. At 11.30 a.m. the lifeboat returned the master to the ship and stood by until the tug took over.

The lifeboat had been at sea for some 20 hours in sub-zero temperatures and appalling conditions, with little protection for the crew against the elements.

Bronze Medal awarded to coxswain **John E. King**

Thanks of the Institution inscribed on vellum awarded to crew-members, **J. Simpson, R. Stott, D. Atkins, G. Traves, F. Walkington, B. Bevan, H.T. Wood, B. Fenton** and **D. Cranswick**.

The M.F.V. *Flamborough Light*

On 16 November 1969 at 6.00 p.m., it was reported that the stern trawler *Flamborough Light*, with a crew of four onboard, had grounded on the harbour sandbar (the Canch) whilst attempting to enter the harbour. Minutes later she was seen drifting out of control outside the South Pier. The weather was cloudy with passing rain squalls, moderate visibility, the wind east-north-east gale force 8, and a rough sea. The lifeboat was launched and proceeded to the position of the casualty, illuminating the area with parachute flares. *Flamborough Light* was seen to be aground, with her stern being pounded by heavy broken seas, just outside the rocky sea defences and sea wall, between the South Pier and the Spa Royal Hall. The lifeboat dropped anchor and veered in towards the casualty, but was unable to get alongside the *Flamborough Light*, because of heavy breaking seas and backwash from the harbour wall. The lifeboat fired a rocket line across to the casualty. Attached to this was a heavy towrope which was then pulled from the lifeboat across to the casualty by her crew. As the tide flowed the lifeboat managed to pull the *Flamborough Light* head to sea and eventually into deeper water. Recovering the lifeboat anchor as they went, the casualty was towed safely into harbour at 8.00 p.m.

The award to John E. King and the lifeboat crew was for determination and brilliant seamanship.

Thanks of the Institution inscribed on vellum awarded to coxswain **John E. King**.

Vellum service certificates were awarded to the rest of the crew: **G. Traves, R. Stott, F. Walkington, A. Ayre, D. Cranswick** and **P. Butterworth**.

The *Flamborough Light* was later towed to Grimsby, where it was found that the rudder had broken off and that the propeller blades were stripped down to the boss.

The *Tiger II*

(Taken from RNLI Records) On 13 September 1970 the alarm was raised, when a small boat trailer and car were found at a launching site south of Bridlington at dusk. A 16-ft long boat, called *Tiger II*, with four men on board, was reported missing. The lifeboat *William Henry and Mary King* was launched. The men had left no message where they were going, only that they had left on a fishing trip. A message was broadcast over the marine VHF Radio by the Humber coastguards to all shipping in the area. The message asked all ships to be on the lookout for a small boat missing from Bridlington. A south-east gale warning was in operation. The lifeboat began searching from South Landing to Flamborough Head, the usual area for small boats fishing. The collier *W.J.H. Wood*, on passage six miles due east of Flamborough Head, reported seeing a small boat burning what appeared to be flares. Given the weather conditions, they agreed to stand by the small boat until the lifeboat arrived. Once in shouting distance of the casualty Coxswain King tried to persuade one of the crew of the small cabin cruiser to attach a towrope. But no one was able to get onto the fore deck of the small boat; they were all suffering from hypothermia and seasickness. Coxswain King manoeuvred the lifeboat into such a position that made it possible to jump off the starboard after deck of the lifeboat onto the fore deck of the cabin cruiser, which was only about two feet square, and wet from breaking waves. The cabin cruiser was pitching violently. Picking my own time I jumped from the lifeboat onto the cabin cruiser knowing there was only two feet in which to stop before slipping straight over the other side of the boat and into the sea. On landing I managed to grab one of the handrails on top of the cabin, which stopped my momentum. The tow rope was thrown to me, which was tied to the Sampson post. A decision was made that I should stay on board the small vessel for the homeward journey, in case the tow rope parted, and also to look after the men on the *Tiger II*. The *Tiger II* was towed back into Bridlington harbour without further incident.

The award was made for the courage and determination shown when jumping onboard the cabin cruiser.

Thanks of the Institution inscribed on vellum awarded to **Fred Walkington.**

Vellum service certificates were awarded to the rest of the crew: coxswain **John E. King, G. Traves, D. Atkins, D. Cranswick, K. Bentley** and **B. Usher**.

The men had decided to return from their fishing trip at 1 p.m. and, unable to retrieve the anchor which was fast on the bottom, they let it go. Their outboard engine would not start and the small boat began to drift out to sea. They had tried to attract attention by burning rags soaked in petrol, but were not seen. Some time after dark, as a last resort, they set fire to their lifejackets to attract the attention of the passing collier *W.J.H. Wood*. They had no radio or flares onboard.

The M.F.V. *My Susanne*

At 4.30 a.m. on 24 January 1972, Flamborough Coastguards alerted Bridlington Honorary Secretary that local fishing boat *My Susanne* was sending out a 'mayday' radio message requiring urgent lifeboat assistance. The engine had failed and she was drifting onshore as the anchor she had put out was not holding the bottom. The wind was southerly force 7 to gale force 8, with a rough sea. On launching the *William Henry and Mary King* under the command of Coxswain John King, the deck lights of the fishing vessel could be seen towards Sewerby Cliffs. To assess the situation, parachute flares were used to illuminate the area around the *My Susanne*; she was aground on the rock scars with the swell breaking heavily around her. As the tide had just turned and was starting to flood, Coxswain King decided to attempt towing the boat off. The lifeboat dropped anchor and veered in towards the casualty through poor sea conditions. It was pitching violently with the seas breaking over the bows and covering the three of us who were working the anchor cable around the Samson post which was just behind the bow of the lifeboat. About 100 yards from the casualty a rocket line was fired, which went right across the boat, and was connected to a strong towrope, which was passed across from the lifeboat to the *My Susanne*. Gradually the bow of the casualty was pulled round, head to sea, but the lifeboat was unable to pull her free from the rocks at this time. The lifeboat began to ground heavily in the broken shallow water, so the towrope was slackened to allow the lifeboat to move off into deeper water. As this was happening the casualty was being pushed around by the tide and sea and was now lying broadside onto the beach and rolling heavily, grinding her bilges on the rocky bottom. Her skipper Mr Robert Ibbotson, senior, expressed his concern for the safety of the crew and thought his boat was lost. Coxswain King reassured him over the radio and with this skipper Ibbotson managed to restart the *My Susanne's* engine, which had been clogged by seaweed. Gradually the lifeboat pulled the casualty's bow back round, head to sea. Coxswain King increased the power of the lifeboat engines to full speed. With the flowing tide and the limited power of the *My Susanne's* engine, the lifeboat pulled her clear. With the relief of being pulled free, the fishing boat kept coming ahead and passed close alongside the port side of the lifeboat, and then changed course to starboard across the bow of the lifeboat. This took the towrope under the lifeboat and fouled the port propeller, stopping the lifeboat's port engine immediately. *My Susanne* cast off her end of the towrope and waited in deeper water. Skipper Ibbotson requested the lifeboat to escort her into the harbour with the concern that their engine might fail again, as it was not running smoothly. We weighed the lifeboat's kedge anchor, pulled the loose ends of the towrope onboard and then at 8.15 a.m. escorted the *My Susanne* with her crew of four (father and three sons) safely into harbour on the starboard engine.

Bar to his Bronze Medal awarded to coxswain **John E. King.**

Thanks of the Institution inscribed on vellum awarded to crew-members: **G. Traves, D. Atkins, R. Stott, F. Walkington, A. Ayre** and **P. Butterworth**.
Each lifeboat crewman was presented with inscribed pewter tankards by Messrs Salvus, Bain and Arnot Ltd Sunderland, insurers in appreciation of this lifeboat service.

The M.F.V. *White Knight*

On 2 April 1973 the wind was blowing force 9 to 10 north-north-east, with a rough sea and heavy swell, visibility down to about half a mile and frequent hail and snow showers. The Flamborough lifeboat had been launched to stand by fishing cobles at Flamborough Head. At 9.30 a.m. several open cobles were known to be at sea. At 10.30 a.m. the Bridlington lifeboat, *William Henry and Mary King*, was launched to stand by the fishing coble *Calaharis* which had been reported by the harbour master (lifeboat deputy launching authority) as fishing off Hornsea. Shortly after launching the lifeboat sighted the small open fishing coble *Moss Rose* which was making heavy weather, the crew manning the pump constantly. Coxswain King decided to stand by the *Moss Rose*. Conditions were so bad for the coble, that it took 40 minutes to make the one-mile journey back into harbour. During this time the Humber radio had received a PAN PAN message from the motor fishing vessel *White Knight* (a PAN PAN message is an urgent message concerning the safety of a ship) stating she was two miles south-south-east of South Smithic buoy, broken down with engine trouble. She was anchored and, although being pounded by heavy seas, did not require assistance at that time. At 11.30 a.m. the lifeboat returned south to search for the *Calaharis*. At 11.40 a.m. the Honorary Secretary, Arthur Dick, advised the lifeboat to proceed and stand by the *White Knight*, who had reported being pounded by heavy seas and dragging her anchor. The Hon. Secretary also requested, when possible, that the Flamborough lifeboat should take over the search for the *Calaharis*. The Bridlington lifeboat altered course to the reported position of the *White Knight*. As we cleared the shelter of the Smithic Sands the drogue (sea anchor) was deployed; the speed was reduced to five knots to avoid broaching in the heavy swell and following sea. The wind had increased to north-north-east force 12 squalling to 14 (recorded at Spurn coastguard station) and hurricane winds. Heavy snow squalls reduced visibility to less than half a mile, and breaking seas engulfed the lifeboat. Just after midday the skipper of the *White Knight* suggested that he and his crew should launch their life raft but Coxswain King requested him not to do this unless they were actually sinking and in immediate danger. Because of the urgency the lifeboat speed was increased, but visibility was greatly reduced by the heavy squalls of snow. At 12.20 p.m. *White Knight* gave a Decca reading of its position, while the lifeboat crew were huddled round the chart, trying to give some protection. We plotted the position on the wet paper that started life as a chart. With seas constantly breaking over the stern of the lifeboat, the position we plotted, with great difficulty, indicated that the casualty was 2½ miles south by west of the lifeboat. The casualty fired distress flares, but visibility was too poor for them to be seen. Flamborough coastguard reported that, by using their radio directional finding equipment in their look-out, the signals from both lifeboat and the fishing vessel were roughly on the same bearing. At 12.50 p.m. the *White Knight* was sighted, lying broadside to the sea and rolling very heavily. Coxswain King asked the skipper his intentions. After a short discussion the skipper agreed to abandon ship with his crew. The lifeboat passed to the leeward of the casualty. The wind had increased and the sea was like a field of white water. The drogue was tripped and the lifeboat turned head to wind. The crewmen and skipper on the casualty were ready to be taken off by the lifeboat. All the fenders were tied onto the port shoulder of the lifeboat; it was Coxswain King's intention, in view of the way the casualty was laid, to run in and make contact with the vessel with our port shoulder just forward of the wheelhouse on the starboard side. On the first run in two survivors managed to scramble across onto the lifeboat and with this the lifeboat pulled away. Again Coxswain King forced the lifeboat in alongside the casualty, and the second two survivors jumped from the casualty onto the lifeboat. During this operation part of the lifeboat's guard rail was pulled away, as it became entangled with the casualty. The third run in was made to take off the skipper. Once again superficial damage was done to the lifeboat, because of the heavy rolling of the casualty. At 1.05 p.m., with all survivors safely onboard the lifeboat, Coxswain King put the lifeboat head to sea. In view of the severe weather, the lifeboat could not make a direct course for Bridlington Harbour, but at reduced speed (when possible) made for Bridlington. The 10½-mile journey took two hours and 40 minutes. By 3.00 p.m. the wind had eased to north-east force 9. The harbour was entered and at 3.50 p.m. all survivors landed safely.

The award for the service was given for the long and arduous rescue in bitterly cold and treacherous conditions, with winds never less than strong gale force 9 and the lifeboat being continually buffeted by heavy seas, which broke constantly over the lifeboat.

Silver Medal awarded to coxswain **John E. King.**

Thanks of the Institution inscribed on vellum to crew-members: **G. Traves, D. Atkins, R. Stott, F. Walkington, A. Ayre** and **K. Bentley**.

The skipper of the *White Knight*, John Grayson, reported later that the boat had been disabled by mechanical failure. When they dropped anchor it failed to hold on the seabed. There was a 30-foot swell, heavy waves were constantly crashing over the deck, the galley door was swept away. All the fishermen put on lifejackets before making the hazardous leap into the lifeboat. Skipper Grayson said he had been a fisherman all his life and had sailed to Iceland in deep-water trawlers but this experience had been the worst he had ever known.

The *Sunnanhav*

(Taken from RNLI records) At 9.00 a.m. on 15 February 1979 Her Majesty's coastguard reported that a German ship, the *Sunnanhav*, was broken down eight miles north-east of Flamborough Head and was being driven by storm-force winds towards the Flamborough headland. Initially the Bridlington lifeboat was asked to stand by but not to launch. Shortly afterwards came the request for immediate launch. In blizzard conditions the *William Henry and Mary King* was lowered down the ice-covered slipway, onto the beach, by use of a check rope. Once on the beach the temperature was -4°C and the wind had been blowing storm force 10 to 11 for 24 hours from the north-east. The blinding snow reduced visibility to a few yards. Launching through the shore break, the lifeboat was constantly pounded by heavy seas, completely swamping the radar. This was fitted under the aft canopy, and was constantly submerged in water, so it failed almost immediately. To avoid the danger of the heavy pounding waves, which were running the full length of the Smithic Sands, the decision was made to take a course round the south end of the Smithic Sands, being the safest route out of the Bay. Before setting a course for the casualty, the lifeboat was being swept constantly by heavy breaking seas, and all the crew clipped on their safety lines. On clearing the Bay we were informed by Humber coastguards that the *Sunnanhav* had regained limited power but was only four or five miles north-east of Flamborough Head and still being driven to the south-west by the weather. The lifeboat continued towards the casualty, constantly being buffeted by the storm-force winds and deep northerly swell. At times the lifeboat was being knocked off course by up to 45 degrees. Navigation by any other means than dead reckoning was impossible. The lifeboat was keeping in contact with the coastguards every half hour, updating them on its progress. A further message from the coastguards advised the lifeboat that the *Sunnanhav* had regained full power and was making for the river Humber to shelter from the worsening weather. Visibility was down to below 50 yards, a westerly course was set to make a land-fall on the high cliffs between Flamborough and Speeton, and then enter Bridlington Bay from a known position, keeping in mind the extremely poor weather on the Smithic Sands. After about two hours a faint outline of cliffs could be seen through the snow showers. As we identified the cliffs as being north of Filey, Second Coxswain, Dennis Atkin, shouted a warning that he had sighted Filey brig. The wheel was put hard over to port. As the lifeboat turned we were struck by a huge breaking sea on our port side, knocking the lifeboat over to starboard, to such a degree that the automatic engine cut out, expecting the lifeboat to capsize. The lifeboat immediately righted herself over to port without capsizing. After a quick check of the crew-members, who had all been clipped on with safety harnesses, the coxswain set a south-easterly course round Flamborough Head and to enter the Bay. Lifeboat mechanic, Rod Stott, had for some time been trying to get a picture on the radar set. He now managed to get a weak picture which assisted with the return passage into Bridlington Bay. It was just after five o'clock in the evening when the lifeboat and crew entered Bridlington harbour with Her Majesty's coastguards manning both piers with life-saving equipment due to the continuing appalling weather. We later discovered that other lifeboats, to the north on the coast, had been unable to launch because of the weather conditions. The Humber lifeboat was also out on service. We re-fuelled the lifeboat in the harbour, with difficulty, as the diesel was freezing in the funnel. To leave the lifeboat in the harbour overnight meant taking the lifeboat off service at low water. There would have been no lifeboat available to launch on this coast. While the lifeboat was being re-fuelled, I went to speak to John Crawford, head tractor driver, and Harry Wood, head launcher. The normal slipway from the road to the beach was impassable through ice and snow, but the Spa slipway, near the South Pier, was reasonably clear of snow and ice, as waves had been crashing over the seawall onto the roadway. The salt water had melted the ice and snow. After the crew had a hot drink and changed into dry clothing, the lifeboat was returned to the South Beach and re-carriaged. With skilful driving by John Crawford and directions by Harry Wood, the carriage and lifeboat was taken along the seafront, up the slipway and turned round in front of the Royal Yorkshire Yacht Club, as the left turn from the Spa slipway towards the lifeboat house was too sharp; it was still covered with ice and snow. The lifeboat was then taken back into the boathouse, being back ready for service 13½ hours after first being called out.

The award was made for courage, leadership and initiative displayed throughout this service.

Bronze Medal awarded to coxswain **Fred Walkington**.

Thanks of the Institution inscribed on vellum to crew-members: **D. Atkins, R. Stott, A. Ayre, P. Staveley, R. Stork** and **C. Sharp**.

Coble *Three Fevers*

(Taken from RNLI records) On 31 January 1980 at 9.20 a.m. the Hon. Secretary, Arthur Dick, advised Coxswain Fred Walkington that five open cobles were at sea. The coble *Renown* was on lee shore half a mile off Rolston with a net in her propeller. The lifeboat was launched immediately. The wind was gale force 8 south-east by east with a heavy easterly swell. Once afloat the lifeboat contacted the coble *Betty A*, by radio, who had managed to get a tow rope to the *Renown* and was towing her slowly back to Bridlington. The lifeboat joined up with the two cobles and escorted them back to harbour at a speed of about four knots. The coble *Three Fevers* was seen offside our position making her way into the Bay. Coastguards passed the latest weather forecast over the radio, north-east winds of 40 knots. On arriving at the harbour, the skipper of the *Renown* reported that he had managed to start his engine and thought it best to try to enter harbour under his own reduced power. He asked the lifeboat to stand-by in case of engine failure. At this point the coble *Three Fevers* steamed over the Canch (sandbank at the end of the North Pier) about 75 yards from the harbour entrance. As we watched, a large sea, estimated to be 12 feet high, crashed over the stern of the *Three Fevers*, filling the coble and washing two of the three crewmen over the side. The coble began to sink by the stern, as fish boxes and pound boards washed out of the boat. The remaining man managed to climb onto the wheelhouse; the air that was trapped in the boat's hull and wheelhouse was keeping the bow of the boat above water. The lifeboat moved in to pull the first man out of the water. He was only just managing to keep afloat and five crewmen on the lifeboat pulled him on board. The second man was being kept afloat by fish boxes, to which he was clinging. The swells had pushed him about 30 feet away from the first man. The lifeboat was manoeuvred towards him and he also was pulled onto the deck of the lifeboat, after some effort as he was a larger man. The third man was still clinging to the *Three Fevers* which was surrounded by nets, ropes and wreckage. A rope was thrown to him which he grabbed. As he entered the water to be pulled on board the lifeboat, a wave crashed over him, pushing him under the water. When he surfaced he still had hold of the rope and was quickly pulled on board the lifeboat. All three men were taken into the harbour and evacuated to hospital by ambulance.

The lifeboat then continued to escort the remaining cobles into harbour; the last coble entered harbour at 3.30 p.m.

The award was made for leadership, skill and determination during this service.

Thanks of the Institution inscribed on vellum to coxswain **Fred Walkington**.

Vellum service certificates awarded to crew-members **D. Atkins, R. Stott, C. Sharp, A. Ayre, P. Staveley** and **H.T. Wood**.

Yacht *Sula Sula*

(Taken from RNLI records) On 11 August 1985 Bridlington coastguard asked for the Bridlington lifeboat *William Henry and Mary King* to be launched as there were several open fishing cobles at sea with angling parties on board. The wind was east by south force 7 causing heavy breaking seas at the harbour entrance and on the beach. The lifeboat took up a position off the harbour entrance, as the cobles approached, then escorted two fishing cobles into harbour; both cobles were carrying 12 anglers. The lifeboat was contacted, over the radio, by Humber coastguards who asked it to proceed to the assistance of fishing coble *Serene* who was standing by a yacht that had been burning red distress flares. The wind had increased to force 7 to 8. The lifeboat proceeded at full speed, and at 3.40 p.m. the *Serene* and the yacht were sighted one mile off Hornsea. The yacht had a small jib sail set, but was making no headway towards Bridlington. I spoke to the skipper of the coble, Peter Screeton, who thought that the yacht had possibly three persons on board, one being a very young child. The sky was now heavily overcast; there was driving rain with poor visibility and a force 8 gale, which was causing ten-foot breaking seas.

The yacht had no radio. Therefore the lifeboat had to manoeuvre alongside the casualty to make any contact. One man and a child were seen in the cockpit of the yacht. The man informed us that there was another young child and a woman below, both of whom were very ill with seasickness. The shore was now too close to waste any time; we would try to tow the yacht off the lee shore and into harbour. Again the lifeboat ran in alongside the yacht, this time telling the man of our intentions, with which he fully agreed. We ran in several times to try to get alongside the casualty, using the engines. The lifeboat was kept alongside the pitching vessel, while the two children and the woman were taken on board the lifeboat. The woman was transferred with difficulty, as she was too ill to help herself. During this operation seas were breaking over both boats, lifting the yacht and throwing it into the lifeboat's guardrails, which were damaged. Running in again, a towrope was passed to the man, who had decided to stay on his yacht. He made the rope fast and the tow back to Bridlington commenced. Constant speed adjustments had to be made as the yacht surged forward on wave crests. The survivors onboard the lifeboat was wrapped in blankets and looked after by the lifeboat crew.

At 4.45 p.m. the yacht was towed safely into Bridlington harbour. The coastguards informed the lifeboat at this time that a coble, with an angling party on board, was breaking up outside the North Pier. The yacht *Sula Sula* and survivors were quickly passed ashore, and the lifeboat then proceeded to sea and stood by in broken water off the North Pier while the RAF helicopter winched up survivors from the fishing coble *Valhalla* which had been wrecked. All those on board the wrecked coble were accounted for, so at 5.25 p.m. the lifeboat escorted another fishing coble into harbour. The lifeboat returned to the beach, re-housed and was ready for service at 7.10 p.m.

The award was made for the skill and judgement shown during this service.

Thanks of the Institution inscribed on vellum to coxswain **Fred Walkington.**

Vellum service certificates awarded to crew-members **A. Ayre, B. Cundall, P. Staveley, H.T. Wood, R. Stork** and **N. Wood**.

Motor Boat and Sailing Dinghy

On 19 October 1986 the ILB was called out, with Andrew Brompton on the helm, to search for a missing 15-ft boat. The wind was west-south-west force 8, a rough sea with poor visibility through frequent rainsqualls. The crew searched for some time without success, refusing to abandon the search in such atrocious conditions for the ILB. Eventually they discovered, off Ulrome, two men drifting in a small boat, which had broken down and was at the mercy of the weather. The two men and their boat were taken safely ashore. The ILB then returned to sea to rescue one man from a small sailing dinghy which had capsized off Skipsea, pitching its crewman into the water. Alongside the dinghy Andrew passed the helm of the ILB to crewman, Clive Rank, and then went into the water to help the single crewman of the dinghy who was encountering some difficulty in trying to right his boat; both men eventually managed this. The sailing dinghy and her single crewman were then safely taken ashore by the ILB.

The award was made to Andrew Brompton in recognition of the seamanship and determination displayed by him when the ILB rescued three people.

Thanks of the Institution inscribed on vellum to helmsman **Andrew Brompton**.

Vellum service certificates awarded to crew-members **Clive Rank** and **Ken Smith.**

Yacht *Lobo*

(Taken from RNLI records) On 11 July 2000, Humber Coastguards reported that a sailing yacht *Lobo* had been buffeted by northerly gale-force winds all night and was requesting assistance to enter Bridlington Harbour. The Bridlington lifeboat *Marine Engineer* launched at 6.40 a.m. Weather conditions at the launch site were northerly winds force 7 with a slight to moderate sea in the shelter of Bridlington Bay. A strong northerly gale had been blowing for two days, producing a heavy sea off Flamborough Head and beyond the Smithic sandbanks. On leaving the beach it was noticed that the revolutions on the starboard engine were reduced. Mechanic Stuart Mckie reported that everything seemed in order but couldn't find a fault. It didn't seem to affect the handling of the lifeboat so we continued.

Shortly after sailing from Denmark with a crew of six, all with sailing experience, the yacht *Lobo* had encountered strong gale-force northerly winds, which had blown her southwards, the weather gradually taking its toll on the crew. By early morning 11 July 2000 the crew were exhausted. At 6.15 a.m., noting the navigational hazards on the chart, the skipper requested assistance, through Humber Coastguards, to enter Bridlington Bay.

As the lifeboat ran down the Bay towards Flamborough Head, contact was made on VHF radio with the *Lobo*, as the course they were on would take them to the south of the Smithic Sands on a much longer passage into the Bay. The narrow passage between the North Smithic buoy and Flamborough Head can be treacherous at certain states of the wind and tide. To the untrained eye large breaking seas would hide the passage between the bank and the head. The Hive, a local tide, runs counter to the main current, meeting the tide flowing out of the Bay head on in the narrow gap, creating large random breaking waves, further complicated by the strong northerly gale. Once we got clear of that area I knew the weather conditions would be marginally better.

At 6.50 a.m., on clearing the shelter of Flamborough Head, we encountered strong northerly gale force 9 winds combined with a heavy 20- to 25-foot swell breaking regularly; heavy frequent showers reduced visibility. Contact had been maintained with the yacht on VHF radio; she was located five miles off Flamborough Head. We approached the yacht to assess the situation; her course was erratic with her mainsail set, but not trimmed, making around six knots. Only one of the crew could be seen, lashed to the tiller in what appeared to be a trance, making no attempt to communicate with us. We later found out that he had been on the helm for over 36 hours and was completely exhausted.

After several attempts to get close enough to pass a heaving line to the yacht, a crew-member appeared from the cabin and crawled slowly along the deck. A heaving line was thrown from the lifeboat across the foredeck of the yacht. He attempted to pull it on board but gave up after pulling in only 8 to 10 feet. He then made the rope fast to the yacht's mast. During these manoeuvres large waves broke over the yacht and the deck of the lifeboat. It became apparent that the yacht crew was unable to help themselves, so I would have to put a crew-member on board the yacht. Preparations were made; crewman Stuart Cundall positioned himself on the outside of the lifeboat's port rail and the other crew-members were on the port side ready to help. I was reluctant to lay alongside, or make contact with the hull in the prevailing weather conditions, fearing serious damage to the yacht and knowing they had five exhausted crew-members, unable to help themselves, below deck.

The erratic course of the yacht, heavy breaking seas, combined with the gale force winds, made it extremely difficult to manoeuvre the lifeboat alongside the yacht. Around 20 attempts were made as large waves broke over the lifeboat, one knocking Stuart Cundall off his feet. Crewmen Andrew Brompton and Stuart Tibbett caught hold of him, pulling him back on board the lifeboat. The wave momentarily pushed the lifeboat within reach of the yacht. Andrew Brompton looked up, saw the yacht's rigging and immediately leapt from the lifeboat towards the yacht. He managed to cling to the outside of the yacht rail with the lower half of his body submerged in the sea. The yacht crew, from exhaustion, were unable to help him at this point. The lifeboat was unable to go close alongside the yacht again, either to transfer another crewman, or to help Andrew, for fear of crushing him between the two boats. Andrew had to make a number of attempts, before he could swing his leg onto the deck. He then pulled himself up and over the rail and on board the yacht. Once on board Andrew gathered the heaving line and started pulling it in, whilst the lifeboat crew paid out the heavy towing rope to the yacht. Andrew had great difficulty pulling the rope onto the yacht; he had used a lot of energy climbing on board the yacht. The lifeboat was manoeuvred ahead of the casualty, which was still sailing an erratic course at the speed of six knots. This eased the load on the towrope for Andrew who was then able to make it fast; the time was 7.40 a.m. With the yacht now safely undertow we asked Andrew if he could lower the sails. Unfortunately they were jammed and alone he was unable to clear them. It was almost low water when the lifeboat towing the yacht sailed back into the lee of Flamborough Head. With insufficient water to enter the harbour, we towed the yacht into relative shelter under the lee of Sewerby Cliffs, where we were able to get the lifeboat alongside the yacht. I transferred two crew-members, mechanic Stuart Mckie and Roland Stork, who managed to free and lower the sail. With the yacht now in safe hands, the two yacht crew-members went below deck to join their friends to rest, closing the hatch behind them. With sufficient flood tide to enter the harbour, the casualty was towed into the harbour at approximately 10.30 a.m. As the yacht was moored alongside in the harbour the yacht crew came on deck from the *Lobo*'s cabin, where most of them had been throughout the last 24 hours. Their smiles and thanks spoke volumes to the lifeboat crew. That was job satisfaction of the highest order.

The awards were made to Coxswain Fred Walkington for his courage, seamanship skills and the professional manner in which the service was carried out. To Andrew Brompton for his courage, bravery and determination when boarding the yacht.

Bar to his Bronze Medal awarded to coxswain **Fred Walkington**.

Bronze Medal awarded to **Andrew Brompton**.

Medal service certificates awarded to crew-members **R. Stork, S. Mckie, S. Tibbett** and **S. Cundall**.

Drowning Child

On 29 July 2001, the wind was westerly force 4 to 5, causing a choppy sea. The ILB had launched to several incidents through the offshore wind, with crew changes from time to time. The crew at the time of this incident was Stuart Tibbett, Mark Crozier and Jonathan Wheelhouse. They were patrolling off the South Shore Holiday Village, when they noticed people waving and shouting. On arriving at the position they found people out of their depth in the water, trying to keep a child above the water. Mark and Jonathan entered the water to support the child and bring him into the ILB. The child was unconscious, blue and foaming at the mouth, with no pulse. Jonathan quickly cleared the airway and Mark started giving mouth-to-mouth resuscitation. One adult was holding onto the ILB Lifelines, unable to swim back to the beach through exhaustion. Stuart on the helm slowly manoeuvred the ILB back towards the beach until the man was able to stand. A helicopter from RAF Leconfield had been called for and a Coastguard Land Rover was also waiting on the beach for the aircraft. The ILB crew had continued mouth-to-mouth on the child, and on getting to the beach the casualty was showing signs of recovery. The Fire Brigade who were standing by for the helicopter gave the child oxygen and the ILB crew assisted. The helicopter took the child to Castle Hill Hospital, Hull, where Luke Walker from Leeds made a full recovery.

The following awards were made for the humanity, promptitude and skill shown, in restoring to life a man.

The Royal Humane Society Resuscitation certificate awarded to **Mark Crozier** and **Jonathan Wheelhouse**. A letter of thanks to helmsman, **Stuart Tibbett**.

The Queen's Golden Jubilee Medal

A medal was struck to commemorate the Queen's Golden Jubilee.

Bridlington lifeboat crew-members that were serving on 6 February 2002, who had completed five full calendar years of service to the RNLI, were awarded The Queen's Golden Jubilee Medal.

The medals were awarded to **Andrew Brompton, Christopher Brompton, David Coverdale, Iain Crawford, Mark Crozier, Brian Cundall, Stuart Cundall, Andrew Day, Stuart McKie, John Roberts, Ken Smith, Paul Staveley, Roland Stork, Duncan Stewart, Stuart Tibbett, Fred Walkington MBE, Grant Walkington, John Wright.**

8

The Organisation, Fund-Raising and the Future

The smooth, efficient running of a lifeboat station is the responsibility of the Operations Manager, until 2001 called the Honorary Secretary, in conjunction with the branch committee. The Divisional Inspector of the RNLI oversees each individual lifeboat station. Throughout the history of the RNLI it has been the inspector's responsibility to look after the seaworthiness of the lifeboats and competence of the lifeboat crews. The station administration officer is in place to deal with all correspondence. All lifeboat stations have at least one deputy launching authority to make important decisions if the Operations Manager cannot be contacted. Historically this was quite frequent, but since the invention of the mobile phone, now quite rare.

The longest serving Honorary Secretary was Charles Gray, the Lloyd's agent for Bridlington. He held the post for 32 years, during eight of which the post was held jointly with Mr H. Royal-Dawson. During Mr Gray's term of office, he witnessed Bridlington changing from a small quiet fishing village into a popular holiday resort, and the lifeboat service moving from horse-drawn launches of the pulling and sailing lifeboat into the tractor-launched, motorised lifeboat. In 1920 Mr Gray was elected to the town council and served as mayor for two years, during which time he became an alderman of the town.

Alfred West had been Honorary Secretary for almost 16 years when he retired. He was in office during the difficult period of intense rivalry between the RNLI and private lifeboats. It is on record that he had been not only a good Secretary but a minister of relief to distressed fishermen within the town.

Arthur Dick, a freelance journalist, was the second longest serving Honorary Secretary at Bridlington, with 16 years' service. Even after his retirement in 1983 he continued to serve as deputy launching authority up to the time of his death. A journalist for over 60 years, in 1972 he received the RNLI's public relations award. In 1981 he was voted Bridlington citizen of the year, and the Institution's 'Thanks on Vellum' were presented to him by the RNLI. When he retired as Honorary Secretary, he was made a Freeman of the Borough of East Yorkshire just before his death in 1984.

Arthur, and Chairman Dr Terry Wilson, had an immense impact on the people connected with Bridlington Lifeboat Station, and its smooth running. I had been on the crew for only two years when in 1967 Arthur took on the task of Honorary Secretary. In 1975 they had confidence in a 29-year-old to take on the task of rebuilding the team after the untimely illnesses of John King and George Traves, first and second coxswains respectively. They supported me without question, guided me when I asked

46. *The RNLI divisional inspector Alan Tate showing the next change in lifejacket for lifeboat crews with Dr Terry Wilson, Chairman of the Branch Committee, the author and Arthur Dick, station honorary secretary.*

for help and never interfered with the running of the boat or the training of the crew. They in turn were given the full support of the RNLI Divisional Inspectors such as Lt Alan Tate, Lt Cdr Harry Teare and Tom Nutman. I worked with six Honorary Secretaries and six Divisional Lifeboat Inspectors. Without question the golden years were the years with Arthur Dick and Dr Terry Wilson. They were well respected throughout the RNLI, in the town and by people far and wide, and not least by all the crew and helpers, described by Dr Wilson as, 'The Bridlington lifeboat family.'

The present lifeboat coxswain is Stuart Mckie. Stuart took over the position in November 2003, when the previous coxswain relinquished the post after three years for personal reasons.

This brought to an end the 150-year tradition of the crews voting for the person they wanted to lead them as coxswain of the lifeboat.

Stuart started on the beach crew in 1985 and joined the lifeboat crew in 1988. On the retirement of Rod. Stott in 1990, he applied for the vacant post, and was successful in becoming the Station Mechanic, becoming Coxswain Mechanic on 1 November 2004. As a full-time employee of the RNLI, he is the first coxswain at Bridlington to be paid to carry out these duties. This ended the 199-year history of volunteer coxswains at this station.

The second coxswain is Stuart Tibbett who until recently owned and skippered a local fishing/angling boat and has held a skipper's ticket since 1995. Stuart joined the lifeboat in August 1991 as a beach crew-member, and was a crew-member and helmsman of the ILB. He was made up to second coxswain in November 2003.

Stuart Mckie is supported by 20 volunteers, who come from all walks of life: a carpenter, factory workers, business people, taxi drivers, a roofer, a plumber, guest house owners, amongst others who make up today's Bridlington lifeboat crews.

Fund-Raising

Since the RNLI was formed in 1824, it has the proud record of being funded by donations and public subscriptions. Suggestions later came from the RNLI's Committee of Management to hold a Lifeboat Day, to raise funds to help in saving lives at sea. Such events were planned to take place once each year. Known as 'Lifeboat Saturday', the first one was organised by Mr C.W. Macara in Manchester in 1891. The collectors wore badges on a ribbon like a medal, showing a lifeboat being rowed. These badges had the letters LBSF, which stood for 'Life Boat Saturday Fund', and the year on them. Collections operated as a separate entity until the end of 1910, when the Flag Day was then absorbed into the main RNLI fund-raising organisation. The lifeboat flag, then a lifeboat – both on a pin – were sold in aid of lifeboats from the end of the First World War. Before that there was the round pin badge, now the stick-on lifeboat. All were sold with one aim: to raise funds with which to save life at sea.

At the Bridlington lifeboat branch AGM on 30 January 1914, it was suggested that the Institution should adopt a 'Lifeboat Flower', a blue cornflower, which had been sold in some inland towns with great success to help RNLI funds. A small committee of ladies was invited to carry out this fund-raising effort in Bridlington.

The first official Bridlington Lifeboat Day took place in July 1914, organised by the branch committee, and headed by the Honorary Secretary, Mr A.J. Parnell. At 7.00 a.m. the lifeboat was pulled by eight horses from the boathouse into Queen Street, where it remained on show all day until 6.00 p.m. Then it was taken to the West End of the harbour and launched to the cheers of the great crowd that had assembled. The collectors were supplied with artificial cornflowers, which they sold for a minimum of one penny each and in many cases a shilling or half a crown was given. Many people in the town, showing their support for the lifeboat, wore the cornflowers. The committee organising the street collections had, as its President, Lady Macdonald. The collectors started at 8.00 a.m. and remained out until the late evening. On the day 87½ gross of cornflowers, which had cost £15 6s. 0d., helped to raise £124 for the funds of the RNLI.

After this wonderful start to the fund-raising, in view of the depression caused by the Great War, it was decided not to hold such an event in 1915. The next Flag Day was in 1916 which made £80 12s 5d.; in 1917 the Flag Day raised £101 2s. 0d. and over 12,000 flags were sold; in 1918, £107 19s. 5d. was raised on flag day.

47. The badge worn by the Life Boat Saturday Fund collectors.

The sterling work in fund-raising by ladies in the town was formally recognised in June 1921. The President of the Bridlington Branch of the RNLI, Col Lloyd-Greame, held a meeting in the Town Hall for the sole purpose of forming a local branch of the Ladies Lifeboat Guild. In his opening address he made a special mention of the excellent work done in the past by the ladies. The second speaker was the Mayor who spoke about their lifeboat and the need for fund-raising to enable the good work to progress. It was resolved that a branch of the Guild be formed in Bridlington and several of the ladies present, including Miss Dennett and Miss Norton, undertook to assist in the formation of such a branch.

The Ladies Lifeboat Guild continued to raise funds for the lifeboat. At the AGM in March 1932 they were credited with raising £94 in one year, a £22 increase on the previous year. It was said the branch was very dependent on the ladies not only for the Guild collections but also for the Flag Day, which had resulted in £65 being raised.

Mr. H Royal-Dawson said the work of the Ladies Lifeboat Guild was most essential to the welfare of the local branch, raising funds by means of concerts, flag days, open days, whist drives and jumble sales. Each year the members of the Guild did valuable work for the good of the Bridlington branch and of the RNLI. Mrs Gray, secretary of the Ladies Lifeboat Guild, thanked the members of the branch committee for their kind references to the Guild and its works. Unfortunately, by March 1938 Bridlington no longer had a Ladies Lifeboat Guild.

The rebirth of the Bridlington Ladies Lifeboat Guild took place on 8 June 1946. Eight members met for tea at the home of Mrs W. H. Stokehill. The officers elected were President Lady Sykes, Vice Presidents Lady Hotham, Lady Macdonald of Sleat, and Mrs B. Wright, Chairman Mrs W. H. Stokehill, Secretary Mrs G. Townsend and the Treasurer Miss G. Sharpe.

The Guild has raised thousands of pounds each year for the benefit of the lifeboat service. All funds, together with all proceeds from coffee mornings, tombolas etc., are used for the saving of life at sea. Today the Guild Officers are Chairman June Chippendale, Vice Chairman Kath Horner, Secretary Margaret Renwick, and Treasurer Elsie Chapman. Many members have won RNLI Gold and Silver awards.

In July 2004 the Guild lost their inspirational leading light, Mary, Lady Macdonald of Sleat, who died at the age of 84. Lady Macdonald joined the Guild in the early 1950s. In 1975 she became its President − always an active president, an inspiration to everyone, working tirelessly as a fund-raiser for the RNLI. She received numerous honours including the highest award given to a voluntary worker, the bar to the RNLI Gold Badge. She will be sadly missed.

In 1969, Mrs Madge Gurnell had the grand idea of forming a Lifeboat Ladies Luncheon Club. There were several luncheon clubs in the town, all with long waiting lists, so she thought it would be good for the Lifeboat Ladies to have one of their own.

It so happened that at the Guild AGM that November three new members were elected to the Guild Committee – Joan Noble, Irene Turner and Audrey Evans. Immediately after the meeting, while they were enjoying a welcome cup of tea, Mrs Gurnell approached the three ladies saying that the Guild Committee had given her permission to ask them to help her form a luncheon club.

At a meeting at the house of Mrs Gurnell, on 2 February 1970, a committee was formed: Organiser Mrs Gurnell; Deputy Organiser and Minute Secretary, Mrs Joan Brown; Secretary, Mrs Joan Noble; Treasurer, Mrs Irene Turner; Speaker Finder, Mrs Audrey Evans; Committee Members, Mrs June Chippendale and Mrs Ida Jacobs.

At that meeting envelopes were addressed and letters were sent to all paid-up members of Bridlington Ladies Lifeboat Guild and interested friends. In all 535 invitations were sent out. A second meeting was arranged for 18 February. Letters of acceptance were sent to 110 members and then a waiting list was opened.

At a third meeting two more members were invited to join the Committee – Mrs Eleanor King (wife of John King the coxswain) and Mrs Adrienne Richardson.

The Committee had a lot of help from Miss Morrison, the Organising Secretary of the North East Region of the RNLI, in forming the club rules, the main one being that members should meet and lunch together and hear talks and raise funds for the RNLI.

The first fund-raising event was an Apple Pie and Cheese Evening held at the home of Mrs Turner at Thwing in May 1970. The cost of the tickets was four shillings (20 pence) and the grand sum of £118 was raised.

The first Lunch was at the Captain's Table on 28 October 1970. It was attended by 105 members, including the Lady Mayoress, Miss Morrison as guest speaker, and Mrs Thelma Cass the Guild Chairman. Hammonds store gave an excellent parade of hats and furs; they also presented each lady with a white carnation. Part of the display was in red, white and blue to represent the lifeboat service. Mrs Joyce Hall did the flower arrangements, which were later raffled. All present at the lunch signed the Visitors Book, which was presented to the Club by Mrs Gurnell's sons.

The Luncheon Club has continued to flourish – and holds several lunches annually from October to April and two fund-raising events, one in November and one in the spring. Flower arrangements or plants are raffled at every lunch and before Christmas, and cards and calendars are sold. Over the years they have had some excellent speakers including Godfrey Talbot, Richard Whitely and well-known local celebrities. At the AGM the RNLI are presented with a cheque and, over the 34 years of its existence, many thousands of pounds have been raised.

The Luncheon Club moved to the *Expanse Hotel* in 1972. An average of 60 ladies attends each lunch. In June 2004 at York Racecourse the Club were presented with a gavel from the RNLI in recognition of the fund-raising the Club has done. Many members have been presented with RNLI Silver Awards.

The RNLI has two souvenir gift shops connected with the Bridlington lifeboat station. Both raise a substantial amount of money each year from gifts connected with, and supplied by, the RNLI Depot in Thirsk. The shop, at the offshore lifeboat house, is open all year round and the second one, which is part of the inshore lifeboat house on the South foreshore, is open from April to October. The shops are run on a rota system staffed entirely by volunteers (presently averaging around 20), who live in Bridlington and surrounding villages. The majority, but not all, are retired from various occupations and, by choosing to give of their time to raise funds through these sales outlets, contribute towards the vital work of the lifeboat crews.

Both shops are visited regularly by supporters of the RNLI locally or from around the country.

One of the early people to sell souvenirs in aid of the RNLI from the lifeboat house was my father, Fred Walkington senior, in 1952, when the souvenirs consisted of such items as ashtrays, pencils, lifeboat-man figures and a small plastic Liverpool type lifeboat. The items were sold from a table at the open doorway of the offshore lifeboat house. Tom Woodhouse and Richard (Dick) Chadwick, two retired fishermen followed, and, among others, then came Douglas (Doug) Gray MM, the only man I knew who could sell ice to Eskimos. One day a delivery van stopped on the forecourts of the lifeboat house, the driver got out and went into the lifeboat house to ask directions to the Post Office on South Marine Drive, which is less than 50 yards from the lifeboat house. Before he left, Doug had sold him a lifeboat sweater and six packs of Christmas cards.

The Future

Today the crews of lifeboats differ greatly from earlier years, when fishermen and professional mariners provided the manpower to crew lifeboats stationed around the coast, as they had from the earliest days. These men brought with them the seamanship, expertise and local knowledge needed for each individual area of the coastline. With the decline of the fishing and maritime industries, people with seamanship skills readily available to man the lifeboats at Bridlington, as with many other lifeboat stations around the coast of the United Kingdom, are getting fewer. The RNLI and Bridlington station now have to rely heavily on people who do not come from maritime backgrounds, but who are still willing to give up their free time to train and volunteer to man the inshore and offshore lifeboats.

The RNLI have been aware of this nationwide problem for some time. They send to lifeboat stations mobile classrooms in which crew-members can be taught basic seamanship, first-aid, navigation, radio and radar operations. Other courses have been held at the RNLI headquarters in Poole, to give the lifeboat crews the best training possible.

The RNLI introduced at each lifeboat station in 2001 a system of training and recording each crewman's capabilities in the form of a Task Book. Each crew-member is trained in the area of work needed to act competently as a crewman onboard the lifeboat, after which a visiting RNLI representative tests him on his ability. If the crew-man passes, his Task Book is signed for that particular piece of work. Each signed-off item builds up his training, knowledge and capability to go to sea as a competent member of the lifeboat crew.

In 2004 the RNLI opened the Lifeboat College, which was built on land adjacent to their headquarters in Poole, Dorset. This new home for RNLI training aims to give the crews, volunteers and staff the highest level of training in order to save lives at sea. The dedicated survival centre delivers essential rescue and survival training: there is a survival pool with a wave maker, live engine workshops, a full wheelhouse mission simulator plus two P.C. simulators and a variety of interactive workshops. The learning resource centre will be the hub for driving the creation and distribution of educational and information resources to all regions and lifeboat stations. This will ensure that everyone has the learning support needed to reach full potential anywhere in the country.

Education and training has long been an integral part of the RNLI's work: reducing the loss of life by changing attitudes and behaviour, targeting young people with the beach safety programme, holding practical safety demonstrations continuing to build links with the fishing industry, promoting sea safety in all media, and also building general awareness of sea safety, in order to raise sufficient funds to enable the RNLI to save lives now and in the future.

The community of Bridlington and its lifeboat station has been proud to play its part in the work of saving life at sea for 200 years. Bridlington lifeboat started life as a vessel for saving the lives of people from wrecks that had run ashore or were seen to be in imminent danger of sinking close to the shore.

As the lifeboat design improved into a sailing and rowing lifeboat, the work in which it was engaged changed. They were able to rescue those in danger further out to sea. Later, when lifeboats were built with engines, the area in which rescues were possible increased.

Radio and then radar greatly assisted contact with casualties, giving the lifeboat crews a better chance than ever before of rescuing or helping those in need at sea. With today's satellite navigation equipment onboard the lifeboat, help is now at hand faster than ever.

During the early years the lifeboat was called on once or twice per year. It might not have to be called on at all in some years, as the service boards which hang round the walls of the lifeboat house show.

During the first 100-year period, from 1853 until 1953, when records were started, the Lifeboat was called out on service 173 times. From 1953 to date the Offshore Lifeboat has been called out on service 665 times. Included in these figures are the 97 launches in 10 years of the *Marine Engineer* from 1995 until 2005, but not shown are the Inshore lifeboat figures from 1966 to date of 344 launches. This shows that today the lifeboats are as important as ever to the men and women who use the sea off the East Yorkshire coastline for work or recreation.

The Bridlington lifeboat has travelled in time from an open wooden boat to today's *Marine Engineer*. Its crew remain prepared to launch into a howling storm, battered constantly by the sea, in order to save life or give help to the mariner of today.

In 200 years the boats have changed, but the men of Bridlington have always maintained the same ideal:

The Sea Shall Not Have Them

The current vision of the RNLI 2004–2005 is,

> 'TO BE RECOGNISED UNIVERSALLY AS THE MOST EFFECTIVE, INNOVATIVE AND DEPENDABLE LIFEBOAT SERVICE.'

Long may Bridlington Lifeboat Station continue to play its part in this unique Institution.

For a vision of the future of the community of Bridlington, its lifeboats and crews, we must take on board these words, which are as true today as the day they were first spoken by the founder of the RNLI, Sir William Hillary:

> *So long as man shall continue to navigate the ocean, and the tempests shall hold their course over its surface, in every age and on every coast, disasters by sea, shipwreck and peril to human life, must inevitably take place; and with this terrible certainty before our eyes, the duty becomes imperative that we should use every means to obviate and to mitigate the disastrous consequences.*

Sir William Hillary February 1823

FRED WALKINGTON. Esq. MBE. 1 January 2005

Appendices

A. Bridlington Lifeboat Coxswains

John Usher (Silver Medal)	1828		
W. Wallis	1853–1866	13 years	
James Stephenson	1866–1881	15 years	
John Robinson	1871		*Harbinger*
W. Clark	1871		*Seagull*
M.W. Clark	1872		*Seagull*
G. Dixon	1881–1883	2 years	
Robert Wallis	1883–1894	11 years	
Robert Hopper	1884		*Harbinger*
George Wallis	1884		*Seagull*
James Williamson	1894–1898	4 years	
Richard Purvis	1884–1998	10 years	*Barmston*
(Silver Medal)	1898–1913	15 years	
George Johnson	1913–1916	3 years	
Harry Hopper	1916–1924	8 years	
Ernest Welburn	1924–1939	15 years	
Thomas Hutchinson	1939–1949	10 years	
Walter Newby	1950–1959	9 years	
George W. Welburn	1959–1965	6 years	
John King (Silver Medal, Bronze Medal and Bar)	1965–1975	10 years	
Fred Walkington (Bronze Medal and Bar)	1975–2000	25 years	
Roland Stork	2000–2003	3 years	
Stuart McKie	2003–to date		

B. Bridlington Lifeboats

LIFEBOAT	PERIOD	LAUNCHES	LIVES SAVED	COST
The first lifeboat's cost met by local subscriptions and Lloyds	1805 – 1824	Unknown	no records	£150
Lifeboat's cost defrayed by the Institution for the Preservation of	1824 – 1853	Unknown	no records	
Life from Shipwreck	1853 – 1865	5	30	
Harbinger (Fishermen's own lifeboat) Donated by Count Gustave Batthyany	1866 – 1886	Unknown	no records	
Robert Whitworth Gift of the City of Manchester RNLI Branch	1865 – 1866	Unknown	no records	£390

Robert Whitworth Gift of Manchester Branch, per *Robert Whitworth*	1866 – 1871	4	16	£242
Seagull Donated by Rev. Lloyd Greame of Sewerby	1871 – 1898	Unknown	no records	£245
John Abbott Legacy of Mr. J. Abbott of Halifax	1871 – 1885	6	2	£263
William John & Frances (O.N. 9) Legacy of Mr W. J. Payne of Reigate	1885 – 1898	16	44	£300
George & Jane Walker Legacy of Mr G. Walker of Southport (O.N.10) at Barmston	1884 – 1898	1	0	£295
O.N.10 moved to Bridlington	1898 – 1899	0	0	
George & Jane Walker Legacy of Mr. G Walker of Southport (O.N.433)	1899 –1931	58	60	£733
Stanhope Smart (O.N.747) Legacy of the late Mr Stanhope Smart of Huddersfield	1931 – 1947	60	53	£3,742
Tillie Morrison, Sheffield (O.N.851) Gift of Mr James Morrison and the late Mr David Morrison of Sheffield, in memory of their sister	1947 – 1952	53	0	£10,573
Tillie Morrison, Sheffield II (O.N.917) Part of legacy of Mr A. Whitaker of Bradford	1953 – 1967	106	36	£14,481
William Henry & Mary King (O.N.980) Legacy of Miss J. G. King of Sutton, Surrey	1967 – 1988	290	83	£33,000
Peggy & Alex Caird (O.N.1124) Legacy of Miss Mildred Caird	1988 – 1995	104	19	£574,084
Marine Engineer (O.N.1169) Funded by Institute of Marine Engineers and other gifts and legacies	1995 – to-date	99	18	£600,000

INSHORE LIFEBOATS

D–92	1966 – 1970	36	49	£ 950
D–188	1971 – 1983	121	91	£ 1,000
The Lords Feoffees D–299	1984 – 1991	147	132	£ 6,500
The Lords Feoffees II D–426	1992 – 2000	226	63	£ 10,000
The Lords Feoffees III D–557	2000 – to-date	62	7	£ 14,110

The full records of the SEAGULL and HARBINGER lifeboats, together with records of the Bridlington lifeboats before 1853, when the Royal National Institution for the Preservation of Life from Shipwreck took over the management of the Station, unfortunately no longer exist.

C. Honorary Secretaries

William Watson	1853 – 1859	6 Years
John Ross	1859 – 1864	5 Years
John T. Watson	1864 – 1867	3 Years
D. R. W. Porritt	1867 – 1875	8 Years
Alfred West	1875 – 1891	16 Years
Colonel Rickaby	1891 – 1892	1 Year
Captain Thomas Atkin	1892 – 1904	12 Years
Alfred J. Parnell	1904 – 1916	12 Years
Charles Gray (joint 1924 – 1932)	1916 – 1948	32 Years
H. Royal Dawson (joint)	1924 – 1932	8 Years
J. M. Deheer	1948 – 1958	10 Years
M. E. Hodgson	1958 – 1966	8 Years
D. W. Walker	1966 – 1967	1 Year
Arthur Dick	1967 – 1983	16 Years
Lt Cdr G. Davey	1983 – 1986	3 Years
A. Edwards	1986 – 1997	11 Years
B. H. Rodgers	1997 – 1998	1 Year
D. Stamford	1998 –	

D. Lifeboat Motor Mechanics

John Petch	1931 – 1941	10 Years
James Robinson	1941 – 1965	24 Years
Roderick Stott	1965 – 1990	25 Years
Stuart McKie	1990 –	

BIBLIOGRAPHY

The Annals of Bridlington (1867–1942): Indexed news cuttings, Bridlington Library.

Barnett, J. R. *Modern Motor - lifeboats* (London; Blackie, 1923)

Ballantyne, R. M. *Battles with the sea* (James Nisbet & Co., 1883)

The Bridlington Free Press (1859–2004): Weekly newspaper

Dawson, Major A. J. *Britain's Lifeboats, the story of a century of heroic service* (London; Hodder and Stoughton, 1923)

Day, J. W. *Tales of the sea* (Hull; Sailors Institute, 1876)

Fawcett, Ralph S. *The Bridlington Lifeboats* (Bridlington; Ralph S. Fawcett, 1985)

The Hull Daily Mail (1885–2004): Daily newspaper

The Hull Advertiser (1803–1840): Weekly newspaper

The Hull Packet (1805–1806): Weekly news sheet

Lewis, Richard *History of the lifeboat and its work* (London; MacMillan, 1874)

Osler, Adrian G. *Mr Greathead's lifeboats* (Tyne and Wear Museums Service, 1990)

Pugh, R.B. (ed.) *The Victoria History of the County of York: East Riding, Volume II* (Oxford University Press 1974)

Smith, Graham *Smuggling in Yorkshire 1700–1850* (Countryside Books, 1994)

Vince, Charles *Storm on the Water* (London; Hodder & Stoughton, 1946)

Whitaker, H.E. *Men of the Storm* (Bridlington; H. E. Whitaker, 1947)

The York Chronicle (1803–1808)

INDEX